قلائد العقيان في اختصار عقيدة ابن حمدان

Qalā'id al-'Iqyān fī Ikhtiṣār 'Aqīdat Ibn Ḥamdān

The Golden Pendant: The Summarized Creed of Ibn Ḥamdān

Muḥammad b. Badr al-Dīn al-Balbāni
(1006-1083H)

Translation
Abū Ibrāhīm John Starling

Edition 1.1, Rajab | February 2021

ISBN: 9798602898552

Table of Contents

بسم الله الرحمن الرحيم

In the name of Allāh, Most Beneficent, Most Merciful.

Preface

After the unexpected reception of Bidāyat al-ʿAbid, it felt only natural to take on a project in Ḥanbali creed. Due to the very limited number of English books on the topic, Ibn Balbān's summarization of Nihāyat al-Mubtadi'īn fī Usūl al-Dīn was the obvious choice. This is because many of the great Ḥanbali masters have commended the author, Ibn Ḥamdān, and his monumental work and transmitted it including the likes of Ibn Rajab, al-Mardāwi, Ibn Najjār, Marʿī al-Karmi, al-Buhūti, al-Saffārīni, al-Ruḥaybāni, and Ibn Mufliḥ.

The summarization of the text by Ibn Balbān has not only received widespread praise but has become the latter generation's golden standard and preferred teaching manual. The great Imām Shaykh ʿAbdullāh b. Ṣūfān al-Qaddūmi said that "the most renowned creed of our latter day scholars is that of the master and educator, Shaykh Badr al-Dīn, famously known as al-Balbāni who summarized it from Nihāyat al-Mubtadi'īn fī Usūl al-Dīn by the Imām, Ibn Ḥamdān". It was also this very book that Imām al-Saffārīni taught to several of his students from Najd as he indicated in the introduction of his book Lawāmiʿ al-Anwār al-Bahiyyah.

For all intents and purposes, Qala'id al-ʿIqyān, as it is most famously known, represents the canonized creed of the Ḥanābilah. In this exquisite summarization, Ibn Balbān captures the most important topics without delving into the details of evidence or scholastic debate. The work is intentionally concise to encourage mastery and memorization and should serve the disciple well on their journey to Allāh and the home of the Hereafter.

About the Author

Shams al-Dīn Abu ʿAbdullāh Muḥammad b. Badr al-Dīn b. Abd al-Qādir b. Muḥammad, b. Balbān al-Baʿli al-Dimishqi al-Khazraji al-Sāliḥi, best known as al-Balbāni, was born in Damascus around 1006H.

He was from the senior most students of al-Shihāb Aḥmad b. Abi al-Wafāʾ al-Wafāʾi in Ḥadīth and Fiqh. Eventually he surpassed his teacher to the point that he was sought after to teach the four schools of Islamic Law. Al-Balbāni issued religious edicts his entire life, was the leading scholar of al-Ṣalihiyah, and had numerous students who would come to him from far and wide.

Imam al-Balbāni commands a very lofty status in the history of Islamic scholarship. He was loved by all. He was recognized as a leading scholar and master of the Islamic sciences.

Al-Muḥibbi said he was "The ḥanbali jurist and scholar of ḥadīth. He was from the Imāms of asceticism... He was a scholar, scrupulous, a worshipper, and spent his time immersed in worship and knowledge; authoring, teaching and learning to the point that Allāh the Most High secured his place in the hearts of both scholar and layman.

He was very religious, righteous, well mannered, and a good companion. He was humble, spoke sweet words, well versed in both religious and worldly matters, and traversed a spiritual path. He would frequently quote from al-Hafiẓ Abu al-Ḥasan Ali b. Aḥmad al-Zaydi [in reference to Zayd b. Ali b. al-Ḥusayn] as was one of his descendants and someone he admired, saying, "Make your voluntary worship as if it was obligatory, sins as if they were acts of disbelief, desires like poison, mixing with people like the fire, and your nourishment like medicine".

He was habitual and very particular. He would leave home to the ʿUmariyyah School in the morning and spend the day there. His time was divided into prayer, reciting the Qur'an, writing, or teaching...

The people of our time have all acknowledged his virtue and leadership. The scholars have many kind and subtle words to say about him.

He was appointed as the khaṭīb of al-Jāmiʿ al-Maẓaffari, better known as Jāmiʿ al-Ḥanābila, which people would deliberately visit for prayers and blessings.

In general, he was the last of those who resembled the pious predecessors while possessing the blessings of the latter generations."

In his book, al-Riyāḍ al-Sundisiyyah fi Talkhīṣ Tārikh al-Ṣaliḥiyyah, Shaykh Muḥammad n. Kinān said that he met with Shaykh al-Islām Muḥammad b. Balbān. The great scholars of the Levant would go to the ʿUmariyyah School in al-Ṣaliḥiyyah to read to him even though there were many scholars in Damascus. So many read to him that the number is uncountable.

There is no scholar today that did not read to him nor receive from him his short chains of ḥadīth narrations.

Imam al-Baʿli said that, "He was the shaykh, the imām, the authority, the mainstay, the scholar, very special for his day and age, none were like him. He was Shaykh al-Islām wa al-Muslimīn, the adornment of the practicing scholars, the mainstay of the researchers, the pinnacle of rigorous scholarship. Muḥammad b. Badr al-Dīn b. ʿAbd al-Qādir b. Balbān al-Khazraji al-Qādiri al-Ḥanbali who possessed many virtuous qualities and a lofty status."

He authored numerous extremely well-written works which have been celebrated by the scholars and widely received by fellow writers. Some of his works include;

Kāfi al-Mubtadi min al-Ṭullāb

Akhṣar al-Mukhtaṣarāt/The Supreme Synopsis

Mukhtaṣar al-Ifādāt fi Rubʿi alʿIbādāt maʿ al-Ādāb wa Ziyādah

Baghyat al-Mustafīd fi ʿIlm al-Tajwīd

Qalā'id al-ʿIqyān fi Ikhtiṣār ʿAqīdat Ibn Hamdān

Al-Risālat fi Ajwibat As'ilat al-Zaydiyyah

Risālat fi Qirā'at ʿĀsim

Al-Ādāb al-Sharʿiyyah

It was said that the number of works he authored and their summarized nature, in comparison to other scholars of similar status, paled in comparison to the knowledge he possessed and for that reason some biographers would not mention them in his biography.

He passed away Wednesday night, the 9th of Rajab the year 1083H. His son Shaykh Abd al-Raḥmān led an enormous congregation in his funeral prayer in al-Jāmiʿ al-Maẓaffari. He was buried at the foot of Mt. Qāsiyūn on the eastern side next to the garden. The burial was attended by many.

May Allāh shower him with mercy.

About Ibn Ḥamdān

Najm al-Dīn the expert jurist and judge Abu ʿAbdullāh b. Abi al-Thanā', Aḥmad b. Ḥamdān b. Shabīb b. Ḥamdān b. Shabīb b. Ḥamdān b. Maḥmūd b. Shabīb b. Ghiyāth b. Sābiq b. Wathāb al-Numayri al-Ḥarrāni was born in 603H in Ḥarrān and eventually settled in Cairo.

His education began in Ḥarrān under the tutelage of al-Ḥāfiẓ ʿAbd al-Qādir al-Rahāwi from whom he learned 15 juz, Abu ʿAbdullāh Ibn Taymiyyah, and others. He also sought knowledge from many of the pious of the city such as Ibn Abi al-Faham, Ibn Jumayʿi, al-Khaṭīb Fakhr al-Dīn, and studied with his uncle Majd al-Dīn.

In Aleppo he learned from al-Ḥāfiz Ibn Khalil. In Damascus he learned from Ibn Ghassān and Ibn Sabbāḥ. In Jerusalem he learned from al-Iwaqi and others.

He had numerous students who sought knowledge from him and completed their studies. Those who narrated from him include al-Ḥārithy, al-Mizzi, Abu al-Fatḥ al-Yaʿmuri, al-Birzāli, and Quṭb al-Dīn ʿAbd al-Karīm.

He was recognized and highly praised by many scholars. Al-Ḥāfiẓ Ibn Rajab said that he excelled in Fiqh and became the reference of the Ḥanbali school. He was well acquainted with the both Uṣūl al-Fiqh and Uṣūl al-Dīn, varying opinions, and literary studies. He authored numerous works.

Al-Ḥāfiẓ al-Dhahabi said that he was an amazing scholar, the mufti of varying denominations... He was a guardian of knowledge.

Many of the works he authored have become authoritative references in the School of Imām Aḥmad. Those who have referenced his works include, Ibn Mufliḥ, ʿAlāʾ al-Dīn al-Mardāwi when authoring al-Inṣāf, relying upon al-Riʿāyat al-Kubrā and al-Riʿāyat al-Ṣughrā, al-Fatūḥi Ibn Najjār, Marʿī al-Karami, al-Buhūti, al-Saffārini, al-Ruḥaybāni, and others. Many of the Ḥanbali masters quoted from his book Nihāyat al-Mubtadiʾīn fi Uṣūl al-Dīn which is the basis of this book.

His works include:

Al-Ījāz fi al-Fiqh ʿalā Madhhab al-Imām Aḥmad b. Ḥanbal

Al-Muʿtamad fi al-Fiqh ʿalā Madhhab al-Imām Aḥmad b. Ḥanbal

Al-Kifāyat fi Sharḥ al-Hidāyah

Nihāyat al-Muram fi Madhahib al-Anām

Sharḥ al-Muqniʿ

Al-Taqrīb Mukhtaṣar al-Mughni

Sharḥ al-Khiraqi

Ṣifat al-Mufti wa al-Mustafti

al-Wāfi fi Uṣūl al-Fiqh

al-Muqnʿi fi Uṣūl al-Fiqh

He passed away on Thursday, the 6th of Ṣafar in the year 695H.

May Allāh shower him with abundant mercy and grant him eternal bliss in the gardens of Paradise.

Introduction

All praise is for Allāh who absolutely exists as proven by the multitude of His magnificent creation, is known by the cessation of His creatures to be eternal and everlasting, who, in being, action, and attribute is far above equal, resemblance, or likeness.

He is The Omnipotent who brought everything into existence with His lofty words, the All-Knowing who is not oblivious of an atom's weight found in the heavens or on earth, and the Forgiving who pardons sin and conceals the sinners most hideous offenses.

Glorified be He as a deity who is far above the perception of imagination, the comprehension on intelligence, and any and every conjuring of the heart or conception of the mind; all are unlike The Possessor of Honor and Majesty.

I praise Him for guiding us to His true faith, the faith of Islām, and leading us to His oneness according to what He has instilled in us of understanding and pursuit.

I send prayers of peace upon our master Muhammad, the inerrant, the infallible, who conveyed for Allāh His grand true foundational legislation to his people, the best nation of all times who continue to strive in the cause of Allāh until it becomes superior, and upon his family and noble leading companions, the foremost in faith, in such a way that lasts the duration of time.

Commendation of the Book and Reason for Summarization

When I came to know that the creed of the great diligent meticulous inquisitive masterful scrupulous ascetic scholar ʿUbayd Allāh b. Muḥammad b. Muḥammad b. Ḥamdān, may Allāh be pleased and please him and make the best of the Gardens his abode, has been well received and venerated, respected and honored—and how could it not, being that it is one of the best creeds,

مُقَدِّمَةٌ

الحَمْدُ لِلَّهِ الَّذِي يُسْتَدَلُّ عَلَى وُجُوبِ وُجُودِهِ بِبَدِيعِ مَصْنُوعَاتِهِ وَيُعْلَمُ وُجُودُ قِدَمِهِ وَبَقَائِهِ بِفَنَاءِ مَخْلُوقَاتِهِ المُنَزَّهِ عَنِ المَثِيلِ وَالنَّظِيرِ وَالشَّبِيهِ فِي ذَاتِهِ وَأَفْعَالِهِ وَصِفَاتِهِ.

القَدِيرِ الَّذِي أَنْشَأَ المَوْجُودَاتِ بِعَلِيِّ كَلِمَاتِهِ العَلِيمِ الَّذِي لَا يَعْزُبُ عَنْ عِلْمِهِ مِثْقَالُ ذَرَّةٍ فِي أَرْضِهِ وَسَمَاوَاتِهِ العَفُوِّ الَّذِي يَعْفُو عَنِ السَّيِّئَاتِ وَيَسْتُرُ عَلَى المُذْنِبِ قَبِيحَ إِسَاءَاتِهِ.

سُبْحَانَهُ مِنْ إِلَهٍ تَنَزَّهَ عَنْ أَنْ تُدْرِكَهُ الأَوْهَامُ أَوْ تُحِيطَ بِهِ العُقُولُ وَالأَفْهَامُ بَلْ كُلُّ مَا خَطَرَ بِالبَالِ أَوْ تَوَهَّمَهُ الخَيَالُ فَهُوَ بِخِلَافِ ذِي الإِكْرَامِ وَالجَلَالِ.

أَحْمَدُهُ أَنْ هَدَانَا لِدِينِهِ الحَقِّ دِينِ الإِسْلَامِ وَأَرْشَدَنَا لِتَوْحِيدِهِ عَلَى حَسَبِ مَا رَكَّبَ فِينَا مِنَ الفَهْمِ وَالإِقْدَامِ.

أُصَلِّي وَأُسَلِّمُ عَلَى سَيِّدِنَا مُحَمَّدٍ المَعْصُومِ عَنِ الزَّيْغِ وَالزَّلَلِ وَكُلِّ مُوهِمٍ نُقْصَانَ المُبَلِّغُ عَنِ اللَّهِ شَرْعَهُ القَوِيمَ العَظِيمَ الأَرْكَانِ إِلَى أُمَّتِهِ خَيْرِ أُمَّةٍ أُخْرِجَتْ لِلنَّاسِ إِلَى آخِرِ الزَّمَانِ فَلَمْ يَزَلْ يُجَاهِدُ فِي اللَّهِ حَتَّى عَلَا دِينُهُ عَلَى سَائِرِ الأَدْيَانِ. وَعَلَى آلِهِ وَصَحْبِهِ السَّادَةِ الأَعْيَانِ وَرُؤَسَاءِ أَهْلِ الإِيمَانِ صَلَاةً دَائِمَةً بَاقِيَةً مَا لَمَحَ الفَرْقَدَانِ وَتَعَاقَبَ الجَدِيدَانِ.

التَّنْوِيهُ بِقِيمَةِ كِتَابِ ابْنِ حَمْدَانَ وَسَبَبُ اخْتِصَارِهِ

وَبَعْدَ لَمَّا رَأَيْتُ عَقِيدَةَ الإِمَامِ العَالِمِ العَامِلِ الزَّاهِدِ الوَرِعِ المُحَقِّقِ المُدَقِّقِ المُتْقِنِ عُبَيْدِ اللَّهِ ابْنِ مُحَمَّدِ بْنِ مُحَمَّدِ بْنِ حَمْدَانَ رَضِيَ اللَّهُ عَنْهُ وَأَرْضَاهُ وَجَعَلَ بُحْبُوحَةَ الجِنَانِ مَسْكَنَهُ وَمَثْوَاهُ قَدْ تَلَقَّيَتْ بِالقَبُولِ وَالتَّعْظِيمِ وَحَظِيَتْ بِالاحْتِرَامِ وَالتَّكْرِيمِ وَكَيْفَ لَا وَهِيَ مِنْ أَنْفَعِ العَقَائِدِ

richest, most beneficial, and comprehensive works despite its lengthiness which has driven most in our time to weariness, proven to be baffling to most of the intellectuals, and decreased the drive of the negligent to commit it to memory—I desired to summarize it to a third of its size.

I have done so to encourage the beginner, promote better understanding, and facilitate its memorization. It is possible that I have made a few small additions for the hopeful benefit of the gnostics.

The original has eight chapters. I have summarized it into five with an epilogue and a postlude.

Chapter One: Awareness of Allāh the Most-High etc.

Chapter Two: Regarding Actions

Chapter Three: Regarding His Rulings/Judgements

Chapter Four: Remaining Traditions and Conditions of The Resurrection

Chapter Five: Prophethood and Leadership

Epilogue: Immensely Important and Unique Benefits

I ask that Allāh make it as beneficial as the original, make it purely for His pleasure, a means to draw near to Him in the gardens of felicity, to protect me from having errored or gone astray, and to grant me success in both statement action regarding that which He is pleased with. I seek success with Him and put my trust in and rely on Him for He suffices me and is the best to trust.

وَأَجَلِّ الْفَوَائِدِ وَأَعْذَبِ الْمَوَارِدِ وَأَجْمَعِ الشَّوَارِدِ إِلَّا أَنَّ فِيهَا تَطْوِيلًا يَمَلُّ مِنْهُ غَالِبُ أَهْلِ هَذَا الزَّمَانِ وَتَعْجَزُ عَنْ إِدْرَاكِ أَفْهَامِ أَكْثَرِ أَهْلِ ذَا الْأَوْهَانِ وَتَقْصُرُ عَنْ حِفْظِهِ هِمَمُ أَهْلِ التَّوَانِ أَحْبَبْتُ اخْتِصَارَهَا إِلَى نَحْوِ ثُلُثِهَا تَرْغِيبًا لِلْمُبْتَدِينَ وَتَقْرِيبًا لِفَهْمِ الطَّالِبِينَ وَتَسْهِيلًا لِتَنَاوُلِ الْحَافِظِينَ وَرُبَّمَا زِدْتُ عَلَيْهَا أَشْيَاءَ رَائِقَةً نَافِعَةً لِأَهْلِ الْمَعْرِفَةِ بَارِقَةً.

وَفِي الْأَصْلِ ثَمَانِيَةُ أَبْوَابٍ فَاخْتَصَرْتُهَا إِلَى خَمْسَةٍ وَخَاتِمَةٍ وَتَتِمَّةٍ.

الْبَابُ الْأَوَّلُ فِي مَعْرِفَةِ اللَّهِ تَعَالَى وَمَا يَتَعَلَّقُ بِذَلِكَ.

الْبَابُ الثَّانِي فِي الْأَفْعَالِ.

الْبَابُ الثَّالِثُ فِي الْأَحْكَامِ.

الْبَابُ الرَّابِعُ فِي بَقِيَّةِ السَّمْعِيَّاتِ وَأَحْوَالِ الْقِيَامَةِ وَغَيْرِ ذَلِكَ.

الْبَابُ الْخَامِسُ فِي النُّبُوَّةِ وَالْإِمَامَةِ.

وَالْخَاتِمَةُ فِي فَوَائِدَ جَلِيلَةٍ وَفَرَائِدَ نَفِيسَةٍ لَا يَسَعُ الْعَاقِلَ الْجَهْلُ بِهَا.

وَاللَّهَ أَسْأَلُ أَنْ يَنْفَعَ بِهَا كَمَا نَفَعَ بِأَصْلِهَا وَأَنْ يَجْعَلَهَا خَالِصَةً لِوَجْهِهِ الْكَرِيمِ مُقَرِّبَةً لَدَيْهِ فِي جَنَّاتِ النَّعِيمِ وَأَنْ يَعْصِمَنِي فِيهَا مِنَ الزَّيْغِ وَالزَّلَلِ وَيُوَفِّقَنِي لِمَا يُرْضِيهِ مِنَ الْقَوْلِ وَالْعَمَلِ وَبِهِ أَنْتَصِرُ وَأَثِقُ وَعَلَيْهِ أَتَوَكَّلُ وَأَعْتَمِدُ وَهُوَ حَسْبِي وَنِعْمَ الْوَكِيلُ.

Chapter 1: Awareness of Allāh the Most-High

It is a legal obligation upon every capable person of legal capacity to be aware of Allāh through examination of existence and creation.

This is the first obligation to The Most-High. If they perish before the call reaches them, the disbeliever will not be punished.

What is intended by being aware of The Most-High is knowing of His absolute existence by way of His perfect and eternal attributes without knowing the reality of His being; an impossibility due to its difference from all of creation.

Awareness of Allāh The Most-High and His attributes is deduced through legislative means. The intellect is the tool of comprehension and discernment.

The first, greatest, and most beneficial faith-based blessing Allāh has bestowed upon the believers is that He has given them the ability to gain awareness of Him, the Glorified and Most-High.

The first of His worldly blessings is a life free from harm.

Thanking the Benefactor is a legal duty which occurs by acknowledging His blessings in a submissive and yielding way and utilizing each blessing in His obedience.

Attributes of Allāh The Most-High

It is obligatory to believe that He, The Most-High, is one who is indivisible and cannot be divided, alone, not of many, unique, the Eternal Refuge, He begets not nor is He begotten, nor is there to Him any equivalent, who has no partner in His dominion, no assistant in bringing things into existence, and no aid in creation, and that there is none like Him in being, attribute, or action.

البَابُ الأَوَّلُ: فِي مَعْرِفَةِ اللهِ تَعَالَى

فَتَجِبُ مَعْرِفَةُ اللهِ تَعَالَى شَرْعًا بِالنَّظَرِ فِي الوُجُودِ وَالمَوْجُودِ عَلَى كُلِّ مُكَلَّفٍ قَادِرٍ.

وَهِيَ أَوَّلُ وَاجِبٍ لَهُ تَعَالَى فَالكَافِرُ أَنْ مَاتَ قَبْلَ أَنْ تَبْلُغَهُ الدَّعْوَةُ لَا يُعَاقَبُ.

وَالمُرَادُ بِمَعْرِفَتِهِ تَعَالَى مَعْرِفَةُ وُجُوبِ وُجُودِ ذَاتِهِ بِصِفَاتِ الكَمَالِ فِيمَا لَمْ يَزَلْ وَلَا يَزَالُ دُونَ مَعْرِفَةِ حَقِيقَةِ ذَاتِهِ لِاسْتِحَالَةِ ذَلِكَ لِأَنَّهَا مُخَالِفَةٌ لِسَائِرِ الحَقَائِقِ.

وَتُحَصَّلُ المَعْرِفَةُ بِاللهِ تَعَالَى وَصِفَاتِهِ شَرْعًا وَالعَقْلُ آلَةُ الإِدْرَاكِ فِيهِ يَحْصُلُ المَيْزُ بَيْنَ المَعْلُومَاتِ.

وَأَوَّلُ نِعَمِ اللهِ تَعَالَى الدِّينِيَّةِ عَلَى المُؤْمِنِ وَأَعْظَمُهَا وَأَنْفَعُهَا أَنْ أَقْدَرَهُ عَلَى مَعْرِفَتِهِ سُبْحَانَهُ وَتَعَالَى.

وَأَوَّلُ نِعَمِهِ الدُّنْيَوِيَّةِ الحَيَاةُ العَرِيَّةُ عَنْ ضَرَرٍ.

وَشُكْرُ المُنْعِمِ وَاجِبٌ شَرْعًا وَهُوَ اعْتِرَافُهُ بِنِعَمِهِ عَلَى جِهَةِ الخُضُوعِ وَالإِذْعَانِ وَصَرْفُهُ كُلَّ نِعْمَةٍ فِي طَاعَتِهِ.

فِي الصِّفَاتِ الوَاجِبَةِ لِلَّهِ تَعَالَى

يَجِبُ الجَزْمُ بِأَنَّهُ تَعَالَى وَاحِدٌ لَا يَتَجَزَّأُ وَلَا يَنْقَسِمُ أَحَدٌ لَا مِنْ عَدَدٍ فَرْدٌ صَمَدٌ لَمْ يَلِدْ وَلَمْ يُولَدْ وَلَمْ يَكُنْ لَهُ كُفُواً أَحَدٌ لَا شَرِيكَ لَهُ فِي مُلْكِهِ وَلَا ظَهِيرَ لَهُ فِي صُنْعِهِ وَلَا مُعِينَ لَهُ فِي خَلْقِهِ لَا مِثْلَ لَهُ فِي ذَاتِهِ وَلَا فِي صِفَاتِهِ وَلَا فِي أَفْعَالِهِ.

He is living, existent, eternal, everlasting, who has no beginning nor initial stage, and no end nor final stage. He, glory to Him the Most-High, is and always will be possessor of His lofty attributes and beautiful names.

As He is the All-Knowing whose knowledge is one, eternal, everlasting, and an integral part of His being which encompasses everything as it is, be it general or specific, there is nothing new that comes to light as things change nor is there something to be added as things multiply and is neither described as common or acquired, nor the result of pondering or investigation.

As He, the Most-High, is capable of all things, whose ability is one, present, eternal, everlasting, an integral part of His being, and connected with everything possible, there is nothing that ever was or will ever be without it.

He, the Most-High, possesses a will which is one, an integral part of His being, eternal, everlasting, and connected with everything possible.

He, the Most-High, is living a life which is one, present, and eternal which is an integral part of His being.

He, the Most-High, hears and sees, with both hearing and sight that is eternal, present, an integral part of His being, and connected with everything heard or seen.

He speaks and converses with speech that is eternal, an integral part of His being, present—not absent—not created, novel, or externally occurring and without similarity, likeness, or defined modality.

حَيٌّ مَوجُودٌ قَدِيمٌ أَزَلِيٌّ لَا أَوَّلَ لَهُ وَلَا بِدَايَةَ وَلَا آخِرَ لَهُ وَلَا نِهَايَةَ لَمْ يَزَلْ وَلَا يَزَالُ سُبْحَانَهُ وَتَعَالَى مُتَّصِفًا بِصِفَاتِهِ العُلْيَا وَأَسْمَائِهِ الحُسْنَى.

وَبِأَنَّهُ عَالِمٌ بِعِلْمٍ وَاحِدٍ قَدِيمٍ بَاقٍ ذَاتِيٍّ مُحِيطٍ بِكُلِّ مَعْلُومٍ كُلِّيٍّ أَوْ جُزْئِيٍّ عَلَى مَا هُوَ عَلَيْهِ فَلَا يَتَجَدَّدُ عِلْمُهُ تَعَالَى بِتَجَدُّدِ المَعْلُومَاتِ وَلَا يَتَعَدَّدُ بِتَعَدُّدِهَا لَيْسَ بِضَرُورِيٍّ وَلَا كَسْبِيٍّ وَلَا نَظَرِيٍّ وَلَا اسْتِدْلَالِيٍّ.

وَبِأَنَّهُ تَعَالَى عَلَى كُلِّ شَيْءٍ قَدِيرٌ بِقُدْرَةٍ وَاحِدٍ وُجُودِيَّةٍ قَدِيمَةٍ بَاقِيَةٍ ذَاتِيَّةٍ مُتَعَلِّقَةٍ بِكُلِّ مُمْكِنٍ فَلَمْ يُوجَدْ شَيْءٌ وَلَا يُوجَدُ إِلَّا بِهَا.

وَبِأَنَّهُ تَعَالَى مُرِيدٌ بِإِرَادَةٍ وَاحِدَةٍ ذَاتِيَّةٍ قَدِيمَةٍ بَاقِيَةٍ مُتَعَلِّقَةٍ بِكُلِّ مُمْكِنٍ.

وَبِأَنَّهُ تَعَالَى حَيٌّ بِحَيَاةٍ وَاحِدَةٍ وُجُودِيَّةٍ قَدِيمَةٍ ذَاتِيَّةٍ.

وَبِأَنَّهُ تَعَالَى سَمِيعٌ بَصِيرٌ بِسَمْعٍ وَبَصَرٍ قَدِيمَيْنِ ذَاتِيَيْنِ وُجُودِيَيْنِ مُتَعَلِّقَيْنِ بِكُلِّ مَسْمُوعٍ وَمُبْصَرٍ.

وَبِأَنَّهُ تَعَالَى قَائِلٌ وَمُتَكَلِّمٌ بِكَلَامٍ قَدِيمٍ ذَاتِيٍّ وُجُودِيٍّ لَا عَدَمِيٍّ غَيْرِ مَخْلُوقٍ وَلَا مُحْدَثٍ وَلَا حَادِثٍ بِلَا تَشْبِيهٍ وَلَا تَمْثِيلٍ وَلَا تَكْيِيفٍ.

The Nature of the Qur'ān

The Qur'ān is the speech of Allāh, His inspiration and revelation, a miracle in and of itself, for all of creation, it is neither created nor does it dwell in anything, and it is not possible to produce some of its verses.

Saying the Qur'ān is Created

Whoever says that the Qur'ān is created, brought into being, or newly made, says that the Qur'ān with my pronunciation or my pronunciation of the Qur'ān is created, brought into being, or newly made, refrains out of doubt, or claims there is someone who can produce its likeness has disbelieved.

Whoever says my pronunciation of the Qur'ān is not created is an innovator. It is obligatory to refrain from such statements and their like due to the predecessors refraining from them and their misleading nature.

Deeming Allāh Free of Created Qualities

It is obligatory to believe that Allāh the Most-High is not a jowhar, jism or 'araḍ, the creation does not dwell in Him, He does not dwell in creation, and is not confined in it.

تَعْرِيفُ الْقُرْآنِ

فَالْقُرْآنُ كَلَامُ اللهِ وَوَحْيُهُ وَتَنْزِيلُهُ مُعْجِزٌ بِنَفْسِهِ لَا بِغَيْرِهِ لِجَمِيعِ الْخَلْقِ غَيْرُ مَخْلُوقٍ وَلَا حَالٍّ فِي شَيْءٍ وَلَا مَقْدُورٍ عَلَى بَعْضِ آيَةٍ مِنْهُ.

حُكْمُ مَنْ قَالَ الْقُرْآنُ مَخْلُوقٌ

فَمَنْ قَالَ الْقُرْآنُ مَخْلُوقٌ أَوْ مُحْدَثٌ أَوْ حَادِثٌ أَوِ الْقُرْآنُ بِلَفْظِي أَوْ لَفْظِي بِالْقُرْآنِ مَخْلُوقٌ أَوْ مُحْدَثٌ أَوْ حَادِثٌ أَوْ وَقَفَ فِيهِ شَاكًّا أَوِ ادَّعَى قُدْرَةَ أَحَدٍ عَلَى مِثْلِهِ كَفَرَ.

وَمَنْ قَالَ لَفْظِي بِالْقُرْآنِ غَيْرُ مَخْلُوقٍ فَهُوَ مُبْتَدِعٌ فَالْوَاجِبُ الْكَفُّ عَنْ هَذِهِ الْعِبَارَاتِ وَمَا يُشْبِهُهَا لِكَفِّ السَّلَفِ عَنْهَا وَلِمَا فِيهَا مِنَ الْإِيهَامِ.

فِي تَنْزِيهِ اللهِ عَنْ سِمَاتِ الْمُحْدَثَاتِ

وَيَجِبُ الْجَزْمُ بِأَنَّ اللهَ تَعَالَى لَيْسَ بِجَوْهَرٍ وَلَا بِجِسْمٍ وَلَا عَرَضٍ وَلَا تَحُلُّهُ الْحَوَادِثُ وَلَا يَحُلُّ فِي حَادِثٍ وَلَا يَنْحَصِرُ فِيهِ.

Affirming a Place for Allah

Whoever believes or says that Allāh, Himself, is everywhere or in a single space is a disbeliever. It is obligatory to believe that He, the Glorified, Most-High, is separate from His creation. Allāh the Most-High existed before space and then created space while existing before its creation. He is not known by the senses nor like humans and His being, attributes, and actions are not subject to comparison.

He has neither spouse nor offspring and is free of need while there is nothing that can do without Him.

Comparison & Anthropomorphism

He is like nothing and nothing is like Him. Whoever likens Him to His creation has disbelieved. This is like one who believes that He the Most-High is a jism unlike other jisms.

The imagination cannot conceive of Him and the mind cannot perceive Him. He does not resemble the creation, and nothing can be compared to Him. He is not known through conjecture. Regardless the case, whatever is conjured in the mind or imagined, He is different, the Lord of Majesty and Honor.

His Names & Attributes are Eternal & Determinate

Allāh the Most-High's names are eternal and determinate. It is therefore not permissible to name or qualify Him except with that found in the Qur'ān, Sunnah, or consensus of this nation's scholars. Regarding interpretations, we are to refrain as they refrained and desist where they desisted. We are not to surpass the Qur'ān, Sunnah, and consensus of the predecessors in that regard.

حُكْمُ مَنْ أَثْبَتَ لِلَّهِ المَكَانَ

فَمَنْ اعْتَقَدَ أَوْ قَالَ إِنَّ اللهَ بِذَاتِهِ فِي كُلِّ مَكَانٍ أَوْ فِي مَكَانٍ فَكَافِرٌ. بَلْ يَجِبُ الجَزْمُ بِأَنَّهُ سُبْحَانَهُ وَتَعَالَى بَائِنٌ مِنْ خَلْقِهِ فَاللَّهُ تَعَالَى كَانَ وَلَا مَكَانَ ثُمَّ خَلَقَ المَكَانَ وَهُوَ كَانَ قَبْلَ خَلْقِ المَكَانِ وَلَا يُعْرَفُ بِالحَوَاسِّ وَلَا يُقَاسُ بِالنَّاسِ وَلَا مَدْخَلَ فِي ذَاتِهِ وَصِفَاتِهِ وَأَفْعَالِهِ لِلْقِيَاسِ.

وَلَمْ يَتَّخِذْ صَاحِبَةً وَلَا وَلَدًا فَهُوَ الغَنِيُّ عَنْ كُلِّ شَيْءٍ وَلَا يَسْتَغْنِي عَنْهُ شَيْءٌ.

حُكْمُ التَّشْبِيهِ وَالتَّجْسِيمِ

وَلَا يُشْبِهُ شَيْئًا وَلَا يُشْبِهُهُ شَيْءٌ فَمَنْ شَبَّهَهُ بِخَلْقِهِ فَقَدْ كَفَرَ كَمَنْ اعْتَقَدَهُ تَعَالَى جِسْمًا أَوْ قَالَ إِنَّهُ جِسْمٌ لَا كَالأَجْسَامِ.

فَلَا تَبْلُغُهُ الأَوْهَامُ وَلَا تُدْرِكُهُ الأَفْهَامُ وَلَا يُشْبِهُ الأَنَامَ وَلَا تُضْرَبُ لَهُ الأَمْثَالُ وَلَا يُعْرَفُ بِالقِيلِ وَالقَالِ وَبِكُلِّ حَالٍ مَهْمَا خَطَرَ بِالبَالِ أَوْ تَوَهَّمَهُ الخَيَالُ فَهُوَ بِخِلَافِ ذِي الإِكْرَامِ وَالجَلَالِ.

أَسْمَاؤُهُ تَعَالَى وَصِفَاتُهُ قَدِيمَةٌ تَوْقِيفِيَّةٌ

أَسْمَاءُ اللَّهِ تَعَالَى وَصِفَاتُهُ قَدِيمَةٌ تَوْقِيفِيَّةٌ فَلَا يَجُوزُ أَنْ نُسَمِّيهِ أَوْ نَصِفَهُ إِلَّا بِمَا وَرَدَ فِي الكِتَابِ أَوِ السُّنَّةِ أَوْ عَنْ جَمِيعِ عُلَمَاءِ الأُمَّةِ فَنَكُفُّ عَمَّا كَفُّوا عَنْهُ مِنَ التَّأْوِيلَاتِ وَنَقِفُ حَيْثُ وَقَفُوا وَلَا نَتَعَدَّى الكِتَابَ وَالسُّنَّةَ وَإِجْمَاعَ السَّلَفِ فِي ذَلِكَ.

Everything that has been authentically reported from Allāh, His messenger ﷺ, or by way of this nation's scholarly consensus must be accepted, applied, and received as is even if the meaning is not comprehended. Interpretation (taʾwīl) or elucidation (tafsīr) of whatever is associated with the Most-High, such as the verses of istiwāʾ, the narration of nuzūl, etc., is therefore impermissible except by that which has been reported from the Prophet ﷺ and some of his companions.

Without exception, this is the way of the predecessors which is the preferred and safer of the two due to its agreement with the forebears of this nation and its preferred scholars—may Allāh be pleased with them all.

We therefore neither say as the Muʿaṭṭilah regarding negation nor are we inclined to the Mumaththilah's deviation regarding affirmation. We affirm and do not distort. We attribute and do not qualify. To have faith in this regard without rejection, negation, comparison, anthropomorphism, or linguistic interpretation is a must.

Discourse regarding the attributes is a branch of discourse regarding the divine being, therefore, just as He has no similarity in being, He has no similarity in attribute.

The existence of His attributes is known while their true essence is not, except by Him the Glorified, Most-High, and we are to refrain from exemplifying their modality.

Our way is the truth between both extremes of falsehood, guidance between both extremes of deviation, which is to affirm the names and attributes while negating comparison and limbs.

فَكُلُّ مَا صَحَّ نَقْلُهُ عَنِ اللهِ أَوْ رَسُولِهِ صَلَّى اللهُ عَلَيْهِ وَسَلَّمَ أَوْ جَمِيعِ عُلَمَاءِ أُمَّتِهِ وَجَبَ قَبُولُهُ وَالْأَخْذُ بِهِ وَإِمْرَارُهُ كَمَا جَاءَ وَإِنْ لَمْ يُعْقَلْ مَعْنَاهُ.

فَيَحْرُمُ تَأْوِيلُ مَا يَتَعَلَّقُ بِهِ تَعَالَى وَتَفْسِيرُهُ كَآيَةِ الِاسْتِوَاءِ وَحَدِيثِ النُّزُولِ وَغَيْرِ ذَلِكَ إِلَّا بِصَادِرٍ عَنِ النَّبِيِّ صَلَّى اللهُ عَلَيْهِ سَلَّمَ أَوْ بَعْضِ الصَّحَابَةِ.

وَهَذَا مَذْهَبُ السَّلَفِ قَاطِبَةً وَهُوَ أَسْلَمُ الْمَذْهَبَيْنِ وَأَوْلَاهُمَا لِمُوَافَقَتِهِ لِسَلَفِ الْأُمَّةِ وَخِيَارِ الْأَئِمَّةِ رِضْوَانُ اللهِ عَلَيْهِمْ أَجْمَعِينَ.

فَلَا نَقُولُ فِي التَّنْزِيهِ كَقَوْلِ الْمُعَطِّلَةِ وَلَا نَمِيلُ فِي الْإِثْبَاتِ إِلَى إِلْحَادِ الْمُمَثِّلَةِ بَلْ نُثْبِتُ وَلَا نُحَرِّفُ وَنَصِفُ وَلَا نُكَيِّفُ فَالْإِيمَانُ بِذَلِكَ وَاجِبٌ مِنْ غَيْرِ رَدٍّ وَلَا تَعْطِيلٍ وَلَا تَشْبِيهٍ وَلَا تَجْسِيمٍ وَلَا تَأْوِيلٍ عَلَى مُقْتَضَى اللُّغَةِ.

وَالْكَلَامُ فِي الصِّفَاتِ فَرْعٌ عَلَى الْكَلَامِ فِي الذَّاتِ فَكَمَا أَنَّهُ لَا شَبِيهَ لَهُ فِي ذَاتِهِ لَا شَبِيهَ لَهُ فِي صِفَاتِهِ فَصِفَاتُهُ مَعْلُومٌ وُجُودُهَا وَلَا يَعْلَمُ حَقَائِقَهَا إِلَّا هُوَ سُبْحَانَهُ وَتَعَالَى وَنَحْنُ نَضْرِبُ عَنْ كَيْفِيَّتِهَا.

فَمَذْهَبُنَا حَقٌّ بَيْنَ بَاطِلَيْنِ وَهُدًى بَيْنَ ضَلَالَتَيْنِ وَهُوَ إِثْبَاتُ الْأَسْمَاءِ وَالصِّفَاتِ مَعَ نَفْيِ التَّشْبِيهِ وَالْأَدَوَاتِ.

Impermissible Names & Attributes

It is impermissible to designate either a name or an attribute to Allāh such as virtuous, cognizant, modest, or expert even if their meanings are correct and confirmed due to the lack of them being reported.

It is also impermissible to address Him in any way that is perceived as deficient, be it a name or attribute, even if it has been reported. Therefore, regarding His lofty reality, the following are not permissible; Māhid, Zāriʿ, Fāliq, etc.

It is neither permissible to name others with the names that are specifically His the Most High like Allāh, al-Raḥmān, al-Ghaffār, al-Malik, al-Ṣamad, al-Mutaʿālī, al-Subbūḥ, al-Quddūs, al-Ilāh, or al-Maʿbūd nor is it for Him to be called upon by other than His beautiful names.

Seeing Allāh

We are certain that the believers will see their Lord, the Most High, with their eyes on the Day of Resurrection and that He the Most High will talk to them; both in a befitting manner. The disbelievers will not see Him.

It is not legally permissible to see Him, Glorified and Most High, in this world while awake, though it is permitted while asleep.

We are certain that while awake, the Prophet ﷺ witnessed His Lord with his own eyes on the night of al-Isrāʾ and spoke to Him directly.

مَا يَحْرُمُ أَنْ يُسَمَّى اللَّهُ بِهِ أَوْ يُوصَفَ

وَيَحْرُمُ أَنْ يُسَمَّى اللَّهُ أَوْ يُوصَفَ بِنَحْوِ فَاضِلٍ وَعَاقِلٍ وَعَارِفٍ وَعَفِيفٍ وَفَقِيهٍ وَإِنْ كَانَ مَعْنَاهُ صَحِيحًا ثَابِتًا لِلَّهِ سُبْحَانَهُ وَتَعَالَى لِعَدَمِ وُرُودِهِ.

وَكَذَلِكَ يَحْرُمُ أَنْ يُطْلَقَ عَلَيْهِ مَا يُوهِمُ نَقْصًا مِن اسْمٍ أَوْ صِفَةٍ وَإِنْ كَانَ وَارِدًا فَلَا يُقَالُ فِي حَقِّهِ تَعَالَى مَاهِدٌ وَلَا زَارِعٌ وَلَا فَالِقٌ وَلَا نَحْوُ ذَلِكَ.

وَيَحْرُمُ أَنْ يُسَمَّى غَيْرُهُ بِأَسْمَائِهِ تَعَالَى الْمُخْتَصَّةِ بِهِ كَاللَّهِ وَالرَّحْمَنِ وَالْغَفَّارِ وَالْمَلِكِ وَالصَّمَدِ وَالْمُتَعَالِي وَالسُّبُّوحِ وَالْقُدُّوسِ وَالإِلَهِ وَالْمَعْبُودِ وَأَنْ يُدْعَى بِغَيْرِ أَسْمَائِهِ الْحُسْنَى.

فِي الرُّؤْيَةِ

وَنَجْزِمُ بِأَنَّ الْمُؤْمِنِينَ يَرَوْنَ رَبَّهُمْ تَعَالَى يَوْمَ الْقِيَامَةِ بِالأَبْصَارِ وَيُكَلِّمُهُمْ عَلَى مَا يَلِيقُ بِهِ تَعَالَى فِيهِمَا وَلَا يَرَاهُ الْكُفَّارُ.

وَلَا تَجُوزُ رُؤْيَتُهُ سُبْحَانَهُ وَتَعَالَى فِي الدُّنْيَا يَقَظَةً شَرْعًا وَتَجُوزُ مَنَامًا.

وَنَجْزِمُ بِأَنَّ النَّبِيَّ صَلَّى اللَّهُ عَلَيْهِ وَسَلَّمَ رَأَى رَبَّهُ لَيْلَةَ الإِسْرَاءِ عِيَانًا يَقَظَةً وَكَلَّمَهُ كِفَاحًا.

Chapter 2: Regarding Actions

Everything besides Allāh and His attributes is created. Allāh the Glorified and Most High created it, brought it into existence, and originated it from nothing, not due to some impulse, benefit, requirement, need, or necessity. It is not binding to take any of that into account regarding any of His actions, the Glorified and High. He the Glorified does not create anything in jest nor is there a creator of jisms, jowhars, ʿaraḍs, or anything else besides Him, the Glorified and Most High.

The Servants' Actions

All the servants' actions are their earnings. They are created by Allāh; the good and evil, the pleasant and repulsive.

The servant is willful and disposed to achieving righteousness and acquiring sin; not coerced, impelled, or obliged.

Allāh the Glorified is the creator of what the servant earns, what he acquires, what he does, the faculty, its object, choice, and the chosen. What is earned refers to the faculty which Allāh creates in the earner according to what they desire to earn. Faculty is the ability to act.

Everything present including the servants' actions along with anything else; Allāh willed their presence even if it be sinful or harmful.

Punishment & Torment of Creation

He the Exalted has the right to torment and punish creation without previous offense, future reward, or suitable appraisal. He the Exalted has the right to do with His creatures as He wills, all of which is fair, and He is not asked about what He does but they are asked.

البَابُ الثَّانِي فِي الأَفْعَالِ

كُلُّ شَيْءٍ سِوَى اللهِ وَصِفَاتِهِ حَادِثٌ وَاللَّهُ سُبْحَانَهُ وَتَعَالَى خَلَقَهُ وَأَوْجَدَهُ وَابْتَدَأَهُ مِنَ العَدَمِ لَا لِعِلَّةٍ وَلَا لِغَرَضٍ وَلَا لِدَاعٍ وَلَا لِحَاجَةٍ وَلَا لِمُوجِبٍ.

وَلَا تَجِبُ رِعَايَةُ ذَلِكَ فِي شَيْءٍ مِنْ أَفْعَالِهِ سُبْحَانَهُ وَتَعَالَى وَلَا يَفْعَلُ سُبْحَانَهُ شَيْئًا عَبَثًا فَلَا خَالِقَ لِجِسْمٍ وَلَا جَوْهَرٍ وَلَا عَرَضٍ وَلَا شَيْءٍ إِلَّا هُوَ سُبْحَانَهُ وَتَعَالَى.

أَفْعَالُ العِبَادِ كَسْبٌ لَهُمْ وَمَخْلُوقَةٌ لِلَّهِ

وَجَمِيعُ أَفْعَالُ العِبَادِ كَسْبٌ لَهُمْ وَهِيَ مَخْلُوقَةٌ لِلَّهِ خَيْرُهَا وَشَرُّهَا حَسَنُهَا وَقَبِيحُهَا.

وَالعَبْدُ مُخْتَارٌ مُيَسَّرٌ فِي كَسْبِ الطَّاعَةِ وَاكْتِسَابِ المَعْصِيَةِ غَيْرُ مُكْرَهٍ وَلَا مُجْبَرٍ وَلَا مُضْطَرٍّ.

وَاللَّهُ سُبْحَانَهُ الخَالِقُ مَا كَسَبَهُ العَبْدُ وَاكْتَسَبَهُ وَفَعَلَهُ وَالقُدْرَةَ وَالمَقْدُورَ وَالاخْتِيَارَ وَالمُخْتَارَ.

وَالكَسْبُ مَا خَلَقَهُ اللَّهُ تَعَالَى فِي مَحَلِّ قُدْرَةِ المُكْتَسِبِ عَلَى وِفْقِ إِرَادَتِهِ فِي كَسْبِهِ.

وَالقُدْرَةُ هِيَ التَّمَكُّنُ مِنَ التَّصَرُّفِ.

وَكُلُّ مَوْجُودٍ مِنْ أَفْعَالِ العِبَادِ وَغَيْرِهَا فَاللَّهُ أَرَادَ وُجُودَهُ وَإِنْ كَانَ مَعْصِيَةً وَمَضَرَّةً.

لَهُ تَعَالَى إِيلَامُ الخَلْقِ وَتَعْذِيبُهُمْ

وَلَهُ تَعَالَى إِيلَامُ الخَلْقِ وَتَعْذِيبُهُمْ مِنْ غَيْرِ جُرْمٍ سَابِقٍ أَوْ ثَوَابٍ لَاحِقٍ أَوْ اعْتِبَارٍ لَائِقٍ فَلَهُ تَعَالَى أَنْ يَفْعَلَ بِخَلْقِهِ مَا شَاءَ وَكُلُّ ذَلِكَ مِنْهُ حَسَنٌ لَا يُسْأَلُ عَمَّا يَفْعَلُ وَهُمْ يُسْأَلُونَ.

He the Glorified and Exalted has the right to expedite or delay reward and punishment and to pardon a sinning Muslim even if they do not repent as well as a disbeliever if they embrace Islām.

The absent are legally addressed when they become present.

Allāh is Not Required to do Anything for His Creation

He is not obliged to do anything for His creation, neither that which is most practical nor that which is most beneficial for them. It is not permissible to say that He created creation to benefit them. Creating the denizens of Hell, eternizing them therein, and the exertion of Iblīs and his army to misguide them etc. is not for their benefit. He is the judge for every ruling.

Comeliness & Repugnance are Determined by Law

Conventional reasoning is pursuant to and coincides with legal texts and thus neither comeliness nor repugnance, gratitude nor denial, praise nor censure, imperative nor prohibition are determined except by the law. Therefore, neither permissibility nor any other ruling are fully known except by way of it. There is no rational ruling for anything which precedes the advent of law.

The Reality of Provision, Guidance, & Misguidance

Allāh is the provider of both ḥalāl and ḥarām. Provision is that in which the living find their sustenance and the finances with which they find benefit.

وَلَهُ سُبْحَانَهُ وَتَعَالَى تَعْجِيلُ الثَّوَابِ وَالعِقَابِ وَتَأْخِيرُهُمَا وَالعَفْوُ عَنِ المُسْلِمِ المُذْنِبِ وَإِنْ لَمْ يَتُبْ وَعَنِ الكَافِرِ إِذَا أَسْلَمَ.

وَالمَعْدُومُ مُخَاطَبٌ إِذَا وُجِدَ.

لَا يَجِبُ عَلَى اللهِ لِخَلْقِهِ شَيْءٌ

لَا يَجِبُ عَلَيْهِ تَعَالَى لِخَلْقِهِ شَيْءٌ وَلَا فِعْلَ الأَصْلَحِ وَالأَنْفَعِ لَهُمْ. وَلَا يَجُوزُ أَنْ يُقَالَ إِنَّمَا خَلَقَ الخَلْقَ لِيَنْفَعَهُمْ فَإِنَّ خَلْقَ أَهْلِ النَّارِ وَتَخْلِيدِهِمْ وَتَسْلِيطِ إِبْلِيسَ وَجُنُودِهِ عَلَيْهِمْ بِالضَّلَالِ وَغَيْرِهِ لَيْسَ لِنَفْعِهِمْ. وَهُوَ الحَاكِمُ بِكُلِّ حُكْمٍ.

التَّحْسِينُ وَالتَّقْبِيحُ مَرَدُّهُ إِلَى الشَّرْعِ

العَقْلُ المَرْعِيُّ تَبَعٌ وَمُوَافِقٌ لِلنَّقْلِ الشَّرْعِيِّ فَلَا حُسْنَ وَلَا قُبْحَ وَلَا شُكْرَ وَلَا كُفْرَ وَلَا مَدْحَ وَلَا ذَمَّ وَلَا أَمْرَ وَلَا نَهْيَ إِلَّا مِنَ الشَّرْعِ فَلَا تُخْتَبَرُ إِبَاحَةٌ وَلَا غَيْرُهَا إِلَّا بِهِ فَلَا حُكْمَ لِلْعَقْلِ فِي عَيْنٍ قَبْلَ وُرُودِ الشَّرْعِ.

حَقِيقَةُ الرِّزْقِ وَالإِضْلَالِ وَالهِدَايَةِ

وَاللهُ هُوَ الرَّزَّاقُ مِنْ حَلَالٍ وَحَرَامٍ وَالرِّزْقُ مَا يَتَغَذَّى بِهِ الحَيُّ وَيَنْتَفِعُ بِهِ مِنَ الأُمُورِ المَالِيَّةِ.

Allāh the Glorified and High misguides whom He wills and guides whom He desires. If He willed, He would surely guide everyone. Whomever Allāh misguides has no guide.

Misguidance is the creation of denial and delusion in the heart, a love for it, and ability to do it.

Guidance is the prescription of faith in the heart, loving it, and the ability to do it. He, the Glorified, is the creator of all creation, the provider of all provision, the granter of life for every living being, the bringer of death to every deceased, the maintainer of what is maintained, and the perisher of that which perishes.

None can repel His rule, fend off His decree, contradict His conclusion, change His decisions, replace what He knows, or remove what He has given in shares.

Between the Possible & Preposterous

Everything which is truly irrational, within the limits of knowledge and reason, is preposterous for Allāh. Hence, Allāh is not described as having the ability to do that which, in the context of His Glory and Loftiness, is absurd such as lying or oppression.

That which is irrational, outside the capacity of knowledge and reason, is not preposterous for Allāh the Most-High such as Him bringing things into existence from nothing and the punishment of the grave and its bliss.

وَاللَّهُ سُبْحَانَهُ وَتَعَالَى أَضَلَّ مَنْ شَاءَ وَهَدَى مَنْ أَرَادَ وَلَوْ شَاءَ اللَّهُ لَجَمَعَهُمْ عَلَى الْهُدَى وَمَنْ يُضْلِلِ اللَّهُ فَمَا لَهُ مِنْ هَادٍ.

وَالإِضْلَالُ خَلْقُ الْكُفْرِ وَالضَّلَالِ فِي الْقَلْبِ وَالْمَحَبَّةِ لِذَلِكَ وَالْقُدْرَةِ عَلَيْهِ.

وَالْهِدَايَةُ كَتْبُ الإِيمَانِ فِيهِ وَتَحْبِيبِهِ وَالْقُدْرَةِ عَلَيْهِ فَهُوَ سُبْحَانَهُ خَالِقُ كُلِّ مَخْلُوقٍ وَرَازِقُ كُلِّ مَرْزُوقٍ وَمُحْيِي كُلِّ حَيٍّ وَمُمِيتُ كُلِّ مَيِّتٍ وَمُبْقِي كُلِّ بَاقٍ وَمُفْنِي كُلِّ فَانٍ.

لَا رَادَّ لِحُكْمِهِ وَلَا صَادَّ عَنْ حَتْمِهِ وَلَا نَاقِضَ لِمَا أَبْرَمَ وَلَا مُغَيِّرَ لِمَا أَحْكَمَ وَلَا مُبَدِّلَ لِمَا عَلِمَ وَلَا مُزِيلَ لِمَا قَسَمَ.

مَا يَسْتَحِيلُ مِنْهُ تَعَالَى وَمَا لَا يَسْتَحِيلُ

وَيَسْتَحِيلُ مِنَ اللَّهِ كُلُّ مَا هُوَ مُسْتَحِيلٌ حَقِيقَةً فِي الْعَقْلِ مِمَّا لِلْعَقْلِ مَدْخَلٌ فِي عِلْمِهِ وَمَجَالٌ فَلَا يُوصَفُ اللَّهُ بِالْقُدْرَةِ عَلَى الْمُحَالِ فِي حَقِّهِ سُبْحَانَهُ وَتَعَالَى كَالْكَذِبِ وَالظُّلْمِ وَنَحْوِهَا.

وَلَا يَسْتَحِيلُ مِنْهُ تَعَالَى مَا هُوَمُسْتَحِيلٌ فِي الْعَقْلِ مِمَّا لَا مَدْخَلَ لِلْعَقْلِ فِي عِلْمِهِ كَإِيجَادِهِ الأَشْيَاءَ مِنْ عَدَمٍ وَعَذَابِ الْقَبْرِ وَنَعِيمِهِ.

Chapter 3: Regarding Rulings

It is obligatory to comply with His decisive commands and refrain from His absolute prohibitions. It is recommended for others. Obedience, submission, and sincerity is required in all.

Virtuous Reward & Just Punishment

The obedient are not entitled to reward from Allāh, nor are the sinners a punishment. The obedient is rewarded by His grace and the sinner is punished because of His fairness. If he is pardoned, it is by His munificence and clemency. Therefore, we are not certain that the obedient will be in Paradise or that the sinner will be in the Hellfire. Rather, we hope for the obedient and fear and hope for the sinner. Legally, the believer's reward and sinner's punishment are everlasting. Whoever performs a good deed and commits a sin, He can reward them for the good and punish them for the sin though it is not incumbent upon Him.

The Nature of Commands & Prohibitions

Legally, as feasible, unrestricted commands and prohibitions are immediate and continual.

The Realities of Islām & Disbelief

Islām is the pronunciation of the shahādatayn with conviction, adhering to the five pillars if obliged, and believing in what the Messenger delivered. Disbelief is denying whatever completes Islām. Whoever commits a major sin or persists with minor sins has acted immorally. Whoever denies an obvious ruling for which decisive consensus has deemed impermissible or permitted or that of absolute evidence such as the impermissibility of swine or the permissibility of bread etc. has disbelieved.

البَابُ الثَّالِثُ فِي الأَحْكَامِ

فَتَجِبُ امْتِثَالُ أَمْرِهِ سُبْحَانَهُ وَاجْتِنَابُ نَهْيِهِ الجَازِمَينَ وَيُسَنُّ فِي غَيْرِهِمَا وَيَلْزَمُ بِهِ الطَّاعَةُ وَالخُضُوعُ وَالإِخْلَاصُ فِي الكُلِّ.

الثَّوَابُ بِفَضْلِهِ وَالعَذَابُ بِعَدْلِهِ

وَلَا يَسْتَحِقُّ المُطِيعُ عَلَى اللهِ ثَوَابًا وَلَا العَاصِي عِقَابًا بَلْ يُثِيبُ الطَّائِعَ بِفَضْلِهِ وَيُعَذِّبُ العَاصِي بِعَدْلِهِ وَإِذَا عَفَا فَبِكَرَمِهِ وَحِلْمِهِ فَلَا نَقْطَعُ لِطَائِعٍ بِجَنَّةٍ وَلَا لِعَاصٍ بِنَارٍ بَلْ نَرْجُو لِلطَّائِعِ وَنَخَافُ عَلَى العَاصِي وَنَرْجُو لَهُ. وَثَوَابُ المُؤْمِنِ وَعِقَابُ الكَافِرِ دَائِمَانِ شَرْعًا وَمَنْ عَمِلَ حَسَنَةً وَسَيِّئَةً فَلَهُ أَنْ يُثِيبَهُ عَلَى حَسَنَتِهِ وَيُعَاقِبَهُ عَلَى سَيِّئَتِهِ وَلَا يَجِبُ ذَلِكَ.

الأَمْرُ وَالنَّهْيُ لِلفَورِ وَالتِّكْرَارِ

الأَمْرُ وَالنَّهْيُ المُطْلَقَانِ لِلفَورِ التِّكْرَارِ المُمْكِنُ شَرْعًا.

حَقِيقَةُ الإِسْلَامِ وَالكُفْرِ

الإِسْلَامُ هُوَ الإِتْيَانُ بِالشَّهَادَتَيْنِ مَعَ اعْتِقَادِهِمَا وَالْتِزَامِ الأَرْكَانِ الخَمْسَةِ إِذَا تَعَيَّنَتْ وَتَصْدِيقُ الرَّسُولِ صَلَّى اللهُ عَلَيْهِ وَسَلَّمَ فِيمَا جَاءَ بِهِ. وَالكُفْرُ جَحْدُ مَا لَا يَتِمُّ الإِسْلَامُ بِدُونِهِ.

وَمَنْ فَعَلَ كَبِيرَةً أَوْ دَاوَمَ عَلَى صَغِيرَةٍ فَسَقَ فَإِنْ جَحَدَ حُكْمًا ظَاهِرًا أُجْمِعَ عَلَى تَحْرِيمِهِ أَوْ عَلَى إِبَاحَتِهِ إِجْمَاعًا قَطْعِيًّا أَوْ ثَبَتَ جَزْمًا كَتَحْرِيمِ لَحْمِ خِنْزِيرٍ أَوْ حِلِّ خُبْزٍ وَنَحْوِهِ كَفَرَ.

Defining Major & Minor Sin

A major sin is that which has a legal punishment associated with it in this life or a threat in the Hereafter. A minor sin is anything besides that.

Whoever disbelieves is requested to repent for a period of three days and then executed if they do not do so.

The Muslim takes after their parents, captor, or country and is required to utter the shahādatayn at the age of puberty if they have not already done so.

It is not said to the immoral: religious, pious, blessed, saved, or saint of Allāh except due to obedience.

The Reality of Faith

Faith is a bond in the heart, a statement upon the tongue, an act of the limbs, and abandonment of sin; it is increased with obedience and diminished, along with its reward, with sin. It is strengthened with knowledge, weakened because of ignorance, heedlessness, and forgetfulness.

The Ruling of "God Willing" In Faith

Regarding it, the statement "God willing" is recommended; not doubting the current state but doubting the outcome or the acceptance of some deeds, due to fear of negligence, or a dislike of self-commendation.

Allāh Decrees Both Good & Evil

Allāh the Most-High decrees both good and evil, benefit and harm, and nothing escapes His decree nor commences without His devisal.

حَدُّ الكَبِيرَةِ وَالصَّغِيرَةِ

وَالكَبِيرَةُ مَا فِيهَا حَدٌّ فِي الدُّنْيَا أَوْ وَعِيدٌ فِي الآخِرَةِ وَالصَّغِيرَةُ مَا عَدَا ذَلِكَ.

وَمَنْ كَفَرَ يُسْتَتَابُ ثَلاثَةَ أَيَّامٍ فَإِنْ لَمْ يَتُبْ قُتِلَ.

وَالمُسْلِمُ تَبَعًا لِأَبَوَيْهِ أَوْ لِسَابِيهِ أَوْ لِلدَّارِ يَلْزَمُهُ الإِتْيَانُ بِالشَّهَادَتَيْنِ إِذَا بَلَغَ إِنْ لَمْ يَكُنْ نَطَقَ بِهِمَا.

وَلَا يُقَالُ لِلْفَاسِقِ دِيِّنٌ وَمُتَّقٍ وَمُوَفَّقٌ وَمُخْلِصٌ وَوَلِيُّ اللهِ إِلَّا بِطَاعَتِهِ.

حَقِيقَةُ الإِيمَانِ

الإِيمَانُ عَقْدٌ بِالجَنَانِ وَقَوْلٌ بِاللِّسَانِ وَعَمَلٌ بِالأَرْكَانِ وَتَرْكُ العِصْيَانِ يَزِيدُ بِالطَّاعَةِ وَيَنْقُصُ هُوَ وَثَوَابُهُ بِالمَعْصِيَةِ وَيَقْوَى بِالعِلْمِ وَيَضْعُفُ بِالجَهْلِ وَالغَفْلَةِ وَالنِّسْيَانِ.

حُكْمُ الاسْتِثْنَاءِ فِي الإِيمَانِ

وَقَوْلُ إِنْ شَاءَ اللهُ فِيهِ سُنَّةٌ لَا عَلَى الشَّكِّ فِي الحَالِ بَلْ فِي المَآلِ أَوْ فِي قَبُولِ بَعْضِ الأَعْمَالِ أَوْ لِخَوْفِ التَّقْصِيرِ أَوْ كَرَاهَةِ تَزْكِيَةِ النَّفْسِ.

اللهُ مُقَدِّرُ الخَيْرِ وَالشَّرِّ

وَاللهُ تَعَالَى مُقَدِّرُ الخَيْرِ وَالشَّرِّ وَالنَّفْعِ وَالضَّرِّ فَلَا يَخْرُجُ شَيْءٌ عَنْ تَقْدِيرِهِ وَلَا يَصْدُرُ إِلَّا بِتَدْبِيرِهِ.

Everything which He knows, decrees, rules in favor of, or makes mention of, its change or contradiction is unimaginable. It is not possible to oppose it and therefore nothing can surpass its appointed time nor precede it, and nothing can change what Allāh has created.

The asphyxiated, murdered, drowned, burned, eaten by wild beast, crucified, killed in wreckage or a fall, etc. is like one who dies at his appointed term in his current condition. There is nothing that can sever anyone's appointed term.

Due to His threat, it is a must that disbelievers remain in Hell eternally and by His promise, others will be removed from it due to the Prophet ﷺ or someone else's intercession, or due to the generosity of the Lord of the worlds either before or after the reprisal but before it concludes in totality.

What Nullifies Sin & Disbelief?

Sins are rendered void with repentance, disbelief with Islām, and obedience with the apostasy associated with death and nothing else.

Obligatory Repentance

Repentance for every sin, be it minor or major, is an obligation upon one of moral capacity to be discharged immediately and is accepted for everything except for associating partners with Allāh.

It is not publicly accepted from a caller to a misguiding innovation, a sorcerer, hypocrite, one who repeatedly apostates, or one who either curses Allāh or His messenger.

The repentant are not to be called wrong-doers or transgressors.

وَكُلُّ مَا عَلِمَهُ أَوْ قَضَاهُ أَوْ حَكَمَ بِهِ أَوْ أَخْبَرَ بِهِ سُبْحَانَهُ لَا يَتَصَوَّرُ تَغْيِيرُهُ وَلَا مُخَالَفَتُهُ وَلَا يُمْكِنُ الخَلَفُ فِيهِ فَلَا يَتَعَدَّى شَيْءٌ أَجَلَهُ وَلَا يَتَقَدَّمُ عَلَيْهِ وَلَا يَتَغَيَّرُ مَا خَلَقَهُ اللَّهُ.

وَالمَخْنُوقُ وَالمَقْتُولُ وَالغَرِيقُ وَالمَحْرُوقُ وَأَكِيلُ الوَحْشِ وَالمَصْلُوبُ وَالمَيِّتُ بِهَدْمٍ أَوْ تَرَدٍّ شِبْهِهِمَا كَمَنْ يَمُوتُ بِأَجَلِهِ عَلَى حَالَتِهِ فَلَا يَقْطَعُ شَيْءٌ أَجَلَ أَحَدٍ.

وَيَجِبُ بِوَعِيدِهِ سُبْحَانَهُ تَخْلِيدُ الكَافِرِ فِي النَّارِ وَبِوَعْدِهِ إِخْرَاجُ غَيْرِهِ مِنْهَا بِشَفَاعَةِ النَّبِيِّ صَلَّى اللَّهُ عَلَيْهِ وَسَلَّمَ أَوْ غَيْرِهِ أَوْ بِكَرَمِ رَبِّ العَالَمِينَ قَبْلَ الاقْتِصَاصِ وَبَعْدَهُ وَقَبْلَ كَمَالِهِ.

بِمَ تُحْبَطُ المَعَاصِي وَالكُفْرُ؟

وَتُحْبَطُ المَعَاصِي بِالتَّوْبَةِ وَالكُفْرُ بِالإِسْلَامِ وَالطَّاعَةُ بِالرِّدَّةِ المُتَّصِلَةِ بِالمَوْتِ وَلَا تُحْبَطُ بِغَيْرِهَا.

التَّوْبَةُ وَاجِبَةٌ وَمِمَّنْ تُقْبَلُ وَمِمَّنْ لَا تُقْبَلُ

وَالتَّوْبَةُ مِنْ كُلِّ ذَنْبٍ صَغِيرٍ أَوْ كَبِيرٍ وَاجِبَةٌ عَلَى المُكَلَّفِ فَوْراً وَتُقْبَلُ فِيمَا عَدَا الشِّرْكُ.

وَلَا تُقْبَلُ ظَاهِراً مِنْ دَاعِيَةٍ إِلَى بِدْعَتِهِ المُضِلَّةِ وَلَا مِنْ سَاحِرٍ وَزِنْدِيقٍ وَهُوَ المُنَافِقُ وَلَا مِمَّنْ تَكَرَّرَتْ رِدَّتُهُ أَوْ سَبَّ اللَّهَ أَوْ رَسُولَهُ.

وَلَا يُقَالُ لِلتَّائِبِ ظَالِمٌ وَلَا مُسْرِفٌ.

The Reality & Conditions of Repentance

It is regret for the sin for the sake of Allāh the Most-High and not for the sake of some worldly benefit or due to people's harassment.

Its requisite is the resolution to avoid committing a potential sin and to restore or replace the injustice, from which repentance is sought, to the deserving, the determination to do so if not possible, and to do so by choice. It is not a requisite to seek pardon of another due to backbiting etc.

It is valid from some sins and not others. Whoever is ignorant of their sin should repent from every sin in general and from those they know of specifically.

Acceptance of repentance is a favor from Allāh.

Its manner is, I am repentant to Allāh for such and such, or, I seek forgiveness from Allāh from it. It is obligatory that either of the two phrases be employed or something like them.

Ḥanbali Issues Pertaining to Repentance

Whoever does not regret committing a punishable sin, the punishment alone is not repentance.

Repentance is valid from an amputee for stealing, a eunuch for illegal fornication, one with a severed tongue from libel, etc.

It is accepted so long as the Angel of Death has not selected the repentant. It is valid from one who has transgressed their repentance so long as they are not determined to repeat the same sin. Whoever neglects the obligatory repentance, while capable of doing so and aware of its obligation must repent for neglecting repentance that time.

حَقِيقَةُ التَّوْبَةِ وَشُرُوطُهَا

وَهِيَ النَّدَمُ عَلَى الذَّنْبِ لِأَجْلِ اللهِ تَعَالَى لَا لِأَجْلِ نَفْعِ الدُّنْيَا أَوْ أَذَى النَّاسِ.

وَشَرْطُهَا العَزْمُ أَلَّا يَعُودَ لِمَعْصِيَةٍ يُمْكِنُهُ فِعْلُهَا وَأَنْ يَرُدَّ المَظْلَمَةَ الَّتِي تَابَ مِنْهَا أَوْ بَدَلَهَا إِلَى مُسْتَحِقِّهَا أَوْ يَعْزِمَ عَلَى ذَلِكَ عِنْدَ العُذْرِ وَأَنْ تَكُونَ عَنْ اخْتِيَارٍ لَا أَنْ يَسْتَحِلَّ مِنْ غِيبَةٍ وَنَحْوِهَا مُطْلَقًا.

وَتَصِحُّ مِنْ بَعْضِ الذُّنُوبِ دُونَ بَعْضٍ وَمَنْ جَهِلَ ذَنْبَهُ تَابَ مُجْمَلًا مِنْ كُلِّ ذَنْبٍ وَخَطِيئَةٍ وَمَا عَلِمَهُ عَيَّنَهُ.

وَقَبُولُ التَّوْبَةِ تَفَضُّلٌ مِنَ اللهِ تَعَالَى وَصِفَتُهَا إِنِّي تَائِبٌ إِلَى اللهِ مِنْ كَذَا أَوْ أَسْتَغْفِرُ اللهَ مِنْهُ فَيَجِبُ الإِتْيَانُ بِإِحْدَى العِبَارَتَيْنِ أَوْ نَحْوِهِمَا.

فِي مَسَائِلَ حَنْبَلِيَّةٍ مِنْ فِقْهِ التَّوْبَةِ

وَمَنْ لَمْ يَنْدَمْ عَلَى مَا حُدَّ بِهِ لَمْ يَكُنْ حَدُّهُ بِمُجَرَّدِهِ تَوْبَةً.

تَصِحُّ تَوْبَةُ الأَقْطَعِ عَنْ السَّرِقَةِ وَالمَجْبُوبِ عَنْ الزِّنَا وَالمَقْطُوعِ اللِّسَانِ عَنْ القَذْفِ وَنَحْوِهِمْ.

وَتُقْبَلُ مَا لَمْ يُعَايِنِ التَّائِبُ مَلَكَ المَوْتِ وَتَصِحُّ مِمَّنْ نَقَضَ تَوْبَتَهُ مَا لَمْ يَعْزِمْ عَلَى مِثْلِ مَا تَابَ مِنْهُ وَمَنْ تَرَكَ التَّوْبَةَ الوَاجِبَةَ مَرَّةً مَعَ القُدْرَةِ عَلَيْهَا وَالعِلْمِ بِوُجُوبِهَا لَزِمَتْهُ التَّوْبَةُ مِنْ تَرْكِ التَّوْبَةِ تِلْكَ المَرَّةَ.

None of those who face the Qiblah disbelieve by sin, even if they commit the major sins so long as they do not permit an obvious ruling which by consensus is impermissible or deny an obvious ruling which by consensus is permissible as eluded to previously.

Eternal Souls

The souls are creations of Allāh the Most-High and whoever says they are eternal has disbelieved.

The Obligatory Belief in Divine Decree & Will

It is obligatory to believe in the divine decree and will; its good and evil, its sweet and bitter, and that whatever befalls the servants will not evade them and whatever evades them will not befall them.

Allāh the Most-High has decreed sin and that which is disliked. He has made it possible and prescribed it for His creation without having commanded it or required them to do it. He prohibited them from it and from being pleased with it. This goes for every impermissible and disliked thing because He is not pleased with disbelief for His servants. He has prohibited immorality, bad conduct, and oppression and made us averse to disbelief, transgression, and sin out of His favor and grace.

Belief in Raqīb & ʿAtīd

It is obligatory to have faith in al-Raqīb and al-ʿAtīd; two angels who have been assigned to the servant to record their deeds, never departing from them; except when in the lavatory as has been said.

وَلا يَكْفُرُ أَحَدٌ مِنْ أَهْلِ القِبْلَةِ بِذَنْبٍ وَإِنْ عَمِلَ الكَبَائِرَ مَا لَمْ يَسْتَحِلَّ حُكْمًا ظَاهِرًا أُجْمِعَ عَلَى تَحْرِيمِهِ أَوْ يَجْحَدَ حُكْمًا ظَاهِرًا أُجْمِعَ عَلَى حِلِّهِ كَمَا تَقَدَّمَ.

كُفْرُ مَنْ قَالَ بِقِدَمِ الأَرْوَاحِ

وَالأَرْوَاحُ مَخْلُوقَةٌ لِلَّهِ تَعَالَى وَيَكْفُرُ القَائِلُ بِقِدَمِهَا.

فِي وُجُوبِ الإِيمَانِ بِالقَضَاءِ وَالقَدَرِ

وَيَجِبُ الإِيمَانُ بِالقَضَاءِ وَالقَدَرِ خَيْرِهِ وَشَرِّهِ حُلْوِهِ وَمُرِّهِ وَأَنَّ مَا أَصَابَ العَبْدَ لَمْ يَكُنْ لِيُخْطِئَهُ وَمَا أَخْطَأَهُ لَمْ يَكُنْ لِيُصِيبَهُ.

وَأَنَّ اللَّهَ تَعَالَى قَضَى المَعَاصِيَ وَالمَكْرُوهَ وَقَدَّرَ ذَلِكَ وَكَتَبَهُ عَلَى خَلْقِهِ وَلَمْ يَأْمُرْهُمْ بِهِ وَلَا أَلْزَمَهُمْ إِيَّاهُ بَلْ نَهَاهُمْ عَنْهُ وَعَنْ الرِّضَا بِهِ وَبِكُلِّ مُحَرَّمٍ وَمَكْرُوهٍ لأَنَّهُ لا يَرْضَى لِعِبَادِهِ الكُفْرَ وَيَنْهَى عَنْ الفَحْشَاءِ وَالمُنْكَرِ وَالبَغْيِ وَكَرَّهَ إِلَيْنَا الكُفْرَ وَالفُسُوقَ وَالعِصْيَانَ فَضْلاً مِنْ اللَّهِ وَنِعْمَةً.

وُجُوبُ الإِيمَانِ بِالرَّقِيبِ وَالعَتِيدِ

وَيَجِبُ الإِيمَانُ بِالرَّقِيبِ وَالعَتِيدِ وَهُمَا مَلَكَانِ مُوَكَّلَانِ بِالعَبْدِ يَكْتُبَانِ أَفْعَالَهُ وَلَا يُفَارِقَانِهِ بِحَالٍ وَقِيلَ بَلْ عِنْدَ الخَلَاءِ.

Chapter 4: Remaining Reports

Belief in the Hour and Its Signs

It is an obligation to have resolute faith in the Last Hour and its signs which include the following: the dajjal, Ya'jūj and Ma'jūj, the descension of Jesus, the appearance of the fire and the beast, the striking, the gathering, and the resurrection of every soul.

The life of the deceased in the grave, being compressed within it, the return of the soul to the body both before and after its annihilation, speaking to Munkar and Nakīr, two angels who enter upon the deceased delivering good news or a warning, and their questioning of the deceased.

The reward and punishment of the deceased is experienced by both body and soul.

The Deceased's Knowledge of Their Visitors

We believe that the deceased knows who visits, which is emphasized on Friday after the sunrise and before sunset.

The Muslims' souls are in the claws of green birds eating in paradise and that the souls of the disbelievers are in the claws of black birds eating in the fire.

And that everyone knows their destination before death.

The Display of the Deceased's Destination

And that the deceased's destination will be displayed to them in the morning and in the evening. If they are from the dwellers of paradise, then it will be from the dwellers of paradise and if they are from the dwellers of the fire, it will be from the dwellers of the fire. It will be said, "This is your destination until Allāh resurrects you on the Day of Resurrection."

البَابُ الرَّابِعُ: بَقِيَّةُ السَّمْعِيَّاتِ

وُجُوبُ الإِيمَانِ بِالسَّاعَةِ وَأَشْرَاطِهَا

فَيَجِبُ الإِيمَانُ جَزْمًا بِالسَّاعَةِ وَأَشْرَاطِهَا مِنَ الدَّجَّالِ وَيَأْجُوجَ وَمَأْجُوجَ وَنُزُولِ عِيسَى وَخُرُوجِ النَّارِ وَالدَّابَّةِ وَالصَّعْقَةِ وَالحَشْرِ وَالنَّشْرِ لِكُلِّ ذِي رُوحٍ.

وَلِإِحْيَاءِ المَيِّتِ فِي قَبْرِهِ وَضَغْطَتِهِ فِيهِ وَرَدِّ رُوحِهِ إِلَى جَسَدِهِ بِعَيْنِهِ قَبْلَ فَنَائِهِ وَبَعْدَهُ وَكَلَامِهِ فِيهِ لِمُنْكَرٍ وَنَكِيرٍ وَسُؤَالِهِمَا لَهُ وَهُمَا مَلَكَانِ يَلِجَانِ عَلَى المَيِّتِ يُبَشِّرَانِهِ أَوْ يُحَذِّرَانِهِ.

وَثَوَابُ المَيِّتِ وَعِقَابُهُ لِلرُّوحِ وَالجَسَدِ.

عِلْمُ المَيِّتِ بِمَنْ يَزُورُهُ

وَنُؤْمِنُ بِأَنَّ المَيِّتَ يَعْلَمُ بِزَائِرِهِ وَيَتَأَكَّدُ ذَلِكَ يَوْمَ الجُمُعَةِ بَعْدَ طُلُوعِ الفَجْرِ وَقَبْلَ طُلُوعِ الشَّمْسِ.

وَبِأَنَّ أَرْوَاحَ المُسْلِمِينَ فِي حَوَاصِلِ طَيْرٍ خُضْرٍ تَعْلُقُ فِي الجَنَّةِ وَأَرْوَاحُ الكُفَّارِ فِي حَوَاصِلِ طَيْرٍ سُودٍ تَعْلُقُ فِي النَّارِ.

وَبِأَنَّ كُلَّ أَحَدٍ يَعْلَمُ مَصِيرَهُ قَبْلَ مَوْتِهِ.

عَرْضُ المَقْعَدِ عَلَى المَيِّتِ

وَبِأَنَّ المَيِّتَ يُعْرَضُ عَلَيْهِ مَقْعَدُهُ بِالغَدَاةِ وَالعَشِيِّ إِنْ كَانَ مِنْ أَهْلِ الجَنَّةِ فَمِنْ أَهْلِ الجَنَّةِ وَإِنْ كَانَ مِنْ أَهْلِ النَّارِ فَمِنْ أَهْلِ النَّارِ يُقَالُ هَذَا مَقْعَدُكَ حَتَّى يَبْعَثَكَ اللهُ إِلَيْهِ يَوْمَ القِيَامَةِ.

The Scale

And that the scale which weighs good and evil deeds is true. It has a pointer and two pans which weighs the scrolls of deeds. Ibn Abbas ﷺ said, "Good deeds will be weighed in the best of ways and evil deeds in the most repugnant of ways."

And that the bodily return after nonexistence is real.

The Reckoning

The Muslims of legal capacity will be called to account except those whom Allāh wills to enter paradise without reckoning. Every person of legal capacity is accountable. Allāh will ask any of the messengers He wishes about conveying the message and any of the disbelievers He wishes about denying the messenger.

The disbelievers are not called to account and so the scrolls of their deeds are not weighed. If a disbeliever does a righteous deed such as making a charitable contribution or freeing a bondservant or is wronged by a Muslim, we hope that their torment will be lessened.

The Ṣirāṭ

We believe that the Ṣirāṭ is real. It is a bridge which extends over Hell and is slippery and unstable. It is sharper than a sword, narrower than a strand of hair, hotter than a coal, and has hooks which grasp the feet.

Traversing it will be in accordance with one's deeds and so there will be those who will walk, ride, or crawl. Both Muslim and disbeliever will pass over it. The believers will cross it like lightening, wind, the finest horses, and riders. The Muslim will be saved and the abraded and clutched will be in the fire.

الإيمَانُ بِالمِيزَانُ

وَبِأَنَّ المِيزَانَ الَّذِي تُوزَنُ بِهِ الحَسَنَاتُ وَالسَّيِّئَاتُ حَقٌّ وَلَهُ لِسَانٌ وَكَفَّتَانِ تُوزَنُ بِهِ صَحَائِفُ الأَعْمَالِ قَالَ ابْنُ عَبَّاسٍ رَضِيَ اللَّهُ تَعَالَى عَنْهُمَا تُوزَنُ الحَسَنَاتُ فِي أَحْسَنِ صُورَةٍ وَالسَّيِّئَاتُ فِي أَقْبَحِ صُورَةٍ. وَبِأَنَّ المَعَادَ الجِسْمَانِيَّ بَعْدَ الإِعْدَامِ حَقٌّ.

فِي الحِسَابِ

وَيُحَاسِبُ المُسْلِمُونَ المُكَلَّفُونَ إِلَّا مَنْ شَاءَ اللَّهُ أَنْ يَدْخُلَ الجَنَّةَ بِغَيْرِ حِسَابٍ وَكُلُّ مُكَلَّفٍ مَسْؤُولٌ وَيَسْأَلُ اللَّهُ مَنْ شَاءَ مِنَ الرُّسُلِ عَنْ تَبْلِيغِ الرِّسَالَةِ وَمَنْ شَاءَ مِنَ الكُفَّارِ عَنْ تَكْذِيبِ الرُّسُلِ.

فَالكُفَّارُ لَا يُحَاسِبُونَ فَلَا تُوزَنُ صَحَائِفُهُمْ وَإِنْ فَعَلَ كَافِرٌ قُرْبَةً مِنْ نَحْوِ صَدَقَةٍ أَوْ عِتْقٍ أَوْ ظَلَمَهُ مُسْلِمٌ رَجَوْنَا لَهُ أَنْ يُخَفَّفُ عَنْهُ العَذَابُ.

وُجُوبُ الإِيمَانِ بِالصِّرَاطِ

وَنُؤْمِنُ بِأَنَّ الصِّرَاطَ حَقٌّ وَهُوَ جِسْرٌ مَمْدُودٌ عَلَى جَهَنَّمَ دَحْضٌ مَزَلَّةٌ أَحَدُّ مِنَ السَّيْفِ وَأَدَقُّ مِنَ الشَّعْرِ وَأَحَرُّ مِنَ الجَمْرِ عَلَيْهِ خَطَاطِيفُ تَأْخُذُ الأَقْدَامَ.

وَأَنَّ عُبُورَهُ بِقَدْرِ الأَعْمَالِ فَمُشَاةً وَرُكْبَانًا وَزُحَّافًا يَمُرُّ عَلَيْهِ المُسْلِمُ وَالكَافِرُ فَيَجُوزُهُ المُؤْمِنُونَ كَالبَرْقِ وَالرِّيحِ وَأَجَاوِدِ الخَيلِ وَالرُّكْبَانِ فَنَاجٍ مُسْلِمٌ وَمَخْدُوشٌ وَمَكْدُوسٌ فِي النَّارِ.

Paradise & Hell

And that both Paradise and Hell are real. They are both created now and what they contain of bliss and punishment was created to last eternity.

The dwellers of Paradise do not urinate or defecate but will exude such an odor as musk.

The Praised Station & The Pond

And that the praised station for our prophet Muḥammad ﷺ is real and true. It is a station of which no other station is greater with Allāh.

And that the pond is real. It is a river whose water is sweeter than honey and whiter than milk.

Its vessels match the number of stars in the sky. The believer will drink from it before they enter Paradise and after they cross the bridge.

Its width is that of a month's journey. Whoever drinks from it once will never go thirsty again. It has two spouts which pour from al-Kawthar.

Remaining Reports

And that the records, the intercession of the prophets, scholars, martyrs, and remaining believers, the exposition, the inquisition, the reckoning, reading of the books, the witness of the limbs and skin, the recompense, and pardon are real and true.

Bringing back the insane and animals is conceivable. The retribution between the children of Ādam and animals, to the degree of an iota, is real and true.

الإِيمَانُ بِالجَنَّةِ وَالنَّارِ

وَبِأَنَّ الجَنَّةَ وَالنَّارَ حَقٌّ وَهُمَا مَخْلُوقَتَانِ الآنَ وَمَا فِيهِمَا مِنْ النَّعِيمِ وَالعَذَابِ خُلِقَتَا لِلْبَقَاءِ.

وَأَهْلُ الجَنَّةِ لَا يَبُولُونَ وَلَا يَتَغَوَّطُونَ بَلْ يَرْشَحُونَ رَشْحًا كَرِيحِ المِسْكِ.

الإِيمَانُ بِالمَقَامِ المَحْمُودِ وَالحَوْضِ

وَبِأَنَّ المَقَامَ المَحْمُودَ لِنَبِيِّنَا مُحَمَّدٍ صَلَّى اللهُ عَلَيْهِ وَسَلَّمَ حَقٌّ وَصِدْقٌ وَهُوَ مَنْزِلَةٌ لَيْسَ عِنْدَ اللهِ أَعْظَمُ مِنْهَا.

وَبِأَنَّ الحَوْضَ حَقٌّ وَهُوَ نَهْرٌ مَاؤُهُ أَحْلَى مِنْ العَسَلِ وَأَشَدُّ بَيَاضًا مِنْ اللَّبَنِ.

آنِيَتُهُ عَدَدُ نُجُومِ السَّمَاءِ يَشْرَبُ مِنْهُ المُؤْمِنُ قَبْلَ دُخُولِهِ الجَنَّةَ وَبَعْدَ جَوَازِهِ الصِّرَاطَ.

عَرْضُهُ مَسِيرَةُ شَهْرٍ مَنْ شَرِبَ مِنْهُ شُرْبَةً لَا يَظْمَأُ بَعْدَهَا أَبَدًا فِيهِ مِيزَابَانِ يَصُبَّانِ مِنْ الكَوْثَرِ.

ذِكْرُ بَقِيَّةِ السَّمْعِيَّاتِ

وَبِأَنَّ الصُّحُفَ وَالشَّفَاعَةَ مِنَ الأَنْبِيَاءِ وَالعُلَمَاءِ وَالشُّهَدَاءِ وَبَقِيَّةِ المُؤْمِنِينَ وَالعَرْضَ وَالمُسَاءَلَةَ وَالحِسَابَ وَقِرَاءَةَ الكُتُبِ وَشَهَادَةَ الأَعْضَاءِ وَالجُلُودِ وَالجَزَاءَ وَالعَفْوَ حَقٌّ وَصِدْقٌ.

وَإِعَادَةُ المَجَانِينَ وَالبَهَائِمِ وَحَشْرُهَا جَائِزٌ.

وَالقِصَاصُ بَيْنَ بَنِي آدَمَ وَسَائِرِ الحَيَوَانَاتِ حَتَّى لِلذَّرَّةِ مِنْ الذَّرَّةِ حَقٌّ وَصِدْقٌ.

Reception of the Book

The audited Muslim will be given their book in their right, the disobedient, in front of them, in their left, and the disbeliever behind their back in their left.

Negation of Contagion and Omens

We believe that there is no contagion, bad omen of birds or owls, rain-producing start, or belly-serpent.

And that the angels, Iblīs, and his evil whisper to incite disbelief, sin, and repugnance are real.

Rulings Regarding the Jinn

And that the devils and ghouls are real and can be seen. Ghouls are sorcerer jinns. ʿUmar ﷺ said, "If you see the ghouls, call the adhān." What he meant was, if you see their shapes, hear their faint voice, or the fire that comes out of them.

In general, the jinn are morally responsible. Like others, according to the nature of their reward, the believers among them will enter Paradise and their disbelievers will enter Hell.

They eat, drink, and marry one another. They have formed bodies and representing figures. Both congregational and Friday prayers are convened with them. A messenger has not come from them.

Their claim of ownership, if Muslim, for what is in their possession is acceptable though their non-believers are treated like combatants.

Oppressing their own race and mankind is impermissible for them. Their slaughtered animals are permissible, and their urine and vomit are pure.

Shaykh al-Islām Ibn Taymiyyah said, "We will see them in Paradise, but they will not see us."

فِي كَيْفِيَّةِ إِعْطَاءِ الكِتَابِ لِلمُسْلِمِ وَالفَاسِقِ وَالكَافِرِ

وَالمُسْلِمُ المُحَاسَبُ يُعْطَى كِتَابَهُ بِيَمِينِهِ وَالفَاسِقُ بِشِمَالِهِ مِنْ أَمَامِهِ وَالكَافِرُ مِنْ وَرَاءِ ظَهْرِهِ بِشِمَالِهِ.

لَا عَدْوَى وَلَا طِيَرَةَ

وَنُؤْمِنُ بِأَنَّهُ لَا عَدْوَى وَلَا طِيَرَةَ وَلَا هَامَةَ وَلَا نَوْءَ وَلَا صَفَرَ.

وَبِأَنَّ المَلَائِكَةَ وَإِبْلِيسَ وَوَسْوَاسَهُ بِالكُفْرِ وَالمَعْصِيَةِ وَالقُبْحِ حَقٌّ.

مَسَائِلُ وَأَحْكَامٌ تَخُصُّ الجِنَّ

وَبِأَنَّ الشَّيَاطِينَ وَالغُولَ حَقٌّ وَتَجُوزُ رُؤْيَتُهُمْ وَالغِيلَانُ سَحَرَةُ الجِنِّ قَالَ عُمَرُ رَضِيَ اللَّهُ عَنْهُ "إِذَا رَأَيْتُمُ الغِيلَانَ فَاهْتِفُوا بِالأَذَانِ" يُرِيدُ رُؤْيَةَ أَشْخَاصِهِمْ أَوْ سَمَاعَ حِسِّهِمْ أَوْ مَا يَخْرُجُ مِنْهُمْ مِنَ النَّارِ.

الجِنُّ مُكَلَّفُونَ فِي الجُمْلَةِ وَيَدْخُلُ مُؤْمِنُهُمُ الجَنَّةَ وَكَافِرُهُمُ النَّارَ كَغَيْرِهِمْ عَلَى قَدْرِ ثَوَابِهِمْ.

وَيَأْكُلُونَ وَيَشْرَبُونَ وَيَتَنَاكَحُونَ وَهُمْ أَجْسَامٌ مُؤَلَّفَةٌ وَأَشْخَاصٌ مُمَثَّلَةٌ وَتَنْعَقِدُ بِهِمُ الجَمَاعَةُ وَالجُمُعَةُ وَلَيْسَ مِنْهُمْ رَسُولٌ.

وَيُقْبَلُ قَوْلُهُمْ أَنَّ مَا بِيَدِهِمْ مُلْكُهُمْ مَعَ إِسْلَامِهِمْ وَكَافِرُهُمْ كَالحَرْبِيِّ.

وَيَحْرُمُ عَلَيْهِمْ ظُلْمُ الآدَمِيِّينَ وَظُلْمُ بَعْضِهِمْ بَعْضًا وَتَحِلُّ ذَبِيحَتُهُمْ وَبَوْلُهُمْ وَقَيْئُهُمْ طَاهِرَانِ.

قَالَ شَيْخُ الإِسْلَامِ ابْنُ تَيْمِيَةَ: وَنَرَاهُمْ فِي الجَنَّةِ وَلَا يَرَوْنَنَا.

Magic & Astrology

We believe that the evil-eye is real, and that magic is true, present, and has an effect. Its teacher and student have disbelieved. The astrologer has disbelieved along with anyone who believes them, deems that the celestial bodies have an effect, the ability for anything, besides Allāh, to create, or deems to possess knowledge of the unseen.

حُكْمُ السِّحْرِ وَالتَّنْجِيمِ

وَنُؤْمِنُ بِأَنَّ العَيْنَ حَقٌّ وَالسِّحْرَ ثَابِتٌ مَوْجُودٌ لَهُ حَقِيقَةٌ يَكْفُرُ مُعَلِّمُهُ وَمُتَعَلِّمُهُ. وَيَكْفُرُ أَيْضًا المُنَجِّمُ وَمَنْ صَدَّقَهُ أَوِ اعْتَقَدَ تَأْثِيرَ النُّجُومِ أَوْ تَأْثِيرَ شَيْءٍ غَيْرَ اللهِ أَوِ اعْتَقَدَ عِلْمَ الغَيْبِ.

Chapter 5: Prophethood & Leadership

It is conceivable that Allāh the Most High could favor His servants by sending them messengers, some more virtuous than others, peace be upon them, to act as intermediaries between them and their Lord, The Generous, The Bountiful.

Unique Qualities of the Prophet ﷺ

We are certain that our Prophet Muḥammad b. ʿAbdullah ﷺ is truly Allāh's messenger to all of man and jinnkind, the seal of the prophets, the best of them, that to him alone belongs the Praised Station, that he was not a follower of his people's religion before the mission but was born a believing Muslim.

The Reality of Miracles

And that decisive and legitimate miracles proving his truthfulness were made manifest to indicate his prophethood in association with his mission work. They are inexplicable statements or actions in association and conjunction with the claim of revelation. They correspond to it and are initiated as a challenge. None can produce them, their like, or anything similar. It is inconceivable that they would appear from a false prophet. We know that he ﷺ was afraid of Allāh's punishment before Allāh secured him from it and that he feared His blame and admonition after that. And that the foundations of His legislation, and all the essentials contained therein have been transmitted to us by way of him with full certainty and that he is infallible regarding what he conveyed for Allāh the Glorified as he is from every sin like all the other prophets, peace be upon them. No one else is infallible. Contradictions between the prophets regarding Allāh's attributes or oneness etc. are unimaginable. Whoever the Prophet ﷺ attested to being in either Paradise or Hell is as he said.

البَابُ الخَامِسُ فِي النُّبُوَّةِ وَالإمَامَةِ

وَيَجُوزُ أَنْ يَتَفَضَّلَ اللَّهُ تَعَالَى بِإِرْسَالِ الرُّسُلِ إِلَى العِبَادِ لِتَكُونَ وَسَائِطَ بَيْنَهُمْ وَبَيْنَ رَبِّهِمُ الكَرِيمِ الجَوَادِ وَبَعْضُهُمْ أَفْضَلُ مِنْ بَعْضٍ صَلَّى اللَّهُ عَلَيْهِمْ وَسَلَّمَ.

مِنْ خَصَائِصِ النَّبِيِّ صَلَّى اللَّهُ عَلَيْهِ وَسَلَّمَ

وَنَجْزِمُ بِأَنَّ نَبِيَّنَا مُحَمَّدَ بْنَ عَبْدِاللَّهِ ﷺ رَسُولُ اللَّهِ حَقًّا إِلَى الجِنِّ وَالإنْسِ كَافَّةً، وَأَنَّهُ خَاتَمُ الأَنْبِيَاءِ وَأَفْضَلُهُمْ، وَأَنَّهُ مَخْصُوصٌ بِالمَقَامِ المَحْمُودِ، وَأَنَّهُ لَمْ يَكُنْ قَبْلَ البَعْثَةِ عَلَى دِينِ قَوْمِهِ، بَلْ وُلِدَ مُسْلِمًا مُؤْمِنًا.

حَقِيقَةُ المُعْجِزَةِ

وَأَنَّ المُعْجِزَةَ القَاطِعَةَ المُعْتَبَرَةَ لِصِدْقِهِ وُجِدَتْ دَالَّةً عَلَى نُبُوَّتِهِ مَقْرُونَةً بِدَعْوَتِهِ وَهِيَ مَا خَرْقُ العَادَةِ مِنْ قَوْلٍ أَوْ فِعْلٍ إِذَا وَافَقَ دَعْوَى الرِّسَالَةِ وَقَارَنَهَا وَطَابَقَهَا عَلَى جِهَةِ التَّحَدِّي ابْتِدَاءً. لَا يَقْدِرُ أَحَدٌ عَلَيْهَا وَلَا عَلَى مِثْلِهَا وَلَا مَا يُقَارِبُهَا وَلَا يَجُوزُ ظُهُورُهَا عَلَى يَدِ كَاذِبٍ بِدَعْوَى النُّبُوَّةِ. وَنَعْلَمُ أَنَّهُ ﷺ كَانَ يَخَافُ عِقَابَ اللَّهِ قَبْلَ أَنْ يُؤْمِنَهُ وَيَخَافُ لَوْمَهُ وَعِتَابَهُ بَعْدَ ذَلِكَ. وَأَنَّ أُصُولَ شَرْعِهِ وَمَا لَا بُدَّ مِنْهُ فِيهِ مَنْقُولٌ إِلَيْنَا مِنْ جِهَتِهِ قَطْعًا وَأَنَّهُ مَعْصُومٌ فِيمَا يُؤَدِّي عَنِ اللَّهِ سُبْحَانَهُ وَكَذَا مِنْ كُلِّ ذَنْبٍ وَكَذَا سَائِرُ الأَنْبِيَاءِ عَلَيْهِ وَعَلَيْهِمُ الصَّلَاةُ وَالسَّلَامُ وَلَا عِصْمَةَ لِغَيْرِهِمْ. وَلَا يَجُوزُ التَّنَاقُضُ مِنَ الأَنْبِيَاءِ فِي صِفَاتِ اللَّهِ تَعَالَى وَوَحْدَانِيَّتِهِ وَنَحْوِ ذَلِكَ. وَمَنْ شَهِدَ لَهُ الرَّسُولُ ﷺ بِجَنَّةٍ أَوْ نَارٍ فَهُوَ كَمَا قَالَ.

The Reality & Rulings of Wonders

Wonders of the saints are real. They are violations of convention; not something which is summoned, does not serve as a challenge, and is not an invitation to their producer nor is that something summoned from him on behalf of him or Allāh.

They do not substantiate the truthfulness of their producer nor the validity of their sainthood, as it could be removed, and they could be a means of their delusion or gradual destruction.

They include both men and women. The saint, for the most part, hides and conceals them. They keep them secret and they are not a source of tranquility, not a reassurance of one's own sainthood, not to be claimed, and due not occur by request but appear as an obvious bestowal of honor upon them. For the most part, neither they, from whom the wonder was produced, nor anyone else, knows that they are one of Allāh's saints.

It is not required to believe someone who claims an authentic wonder without clear evidence or obvious proof which results in certainty even if they were to walk on water, fly in the sky, or subjugate the jinn and beasts of prey until we examine the end of their life and their agreement with the law in regards to what they enjoined and forbade.

If it is found with someone ignorant, it is a trick and deception from Iblīs; it is misleading and a form of misguidance.

There is no fault upon one who assumes the best of someone in whom he sees righteousness for positive assumptions of religious people is good.

The Best of Creation

The prophets are more virtuous than the saints; both are more virtuous than the angels.

حَقِيقَةُ الكَرَامَةِ وَبَعْضِ أَحْكَامِهَا

وَكَرَامَاتُ الأَوْلِيَاءِ حَقٌّ وَهِيَ خَرْقُ العَادَةِ لَا عَلَى وَجْهِ الاسْتِدْعَاءِ لَهَا وَالتَّحَدِّي بِهَا وَالدُّعَاءِ إِلَيْهِ وَلَا عِنْدَ اسْتِدْعَاءِ ذَلِكَ مِنْهُ عَنْ نَفْسِهِ أَوْ عَنِ اللهِ.

وَلَا تَدُلُّ عَلَى صِدْقِ مَنْ ظَهَرَتْ عَلَى يَدَيْهِ وَلَا عَلَى وِلَايَتِهِ لِجَوَازِ سَلْبِهَا وَأَنْ تَكُونَ مَكْرًا وَاسْتِدْرَاجًا بِهِ.

وَتَعُمُّ الرِّجَالَ وَالنِّسَاءَ وَالوَلِيُّ يَكْتُمُهَا وَيَسْتُرُهَا غَالِبًا وَيُسِرُّهَا وَلَا يُسَاكِنُهَا وَلَا يَقْطَعُ هُوَ بِكَرَامَتِهِ بِهَا وَلَا يَدَّعِيهَا وَتَظْهَرُ بِلَا طَلَبِهِ تَشْرِيفًا لَهُ ظَاهِرًا وَلَا يَعْلَمُ مَنْ ظَهَرَتْ مِنْهُ أَوْ غَيْرُهُ أَنَّهُ وَلِيُّ اللهِ تَعَالَى غَالِبًا بِذَلِكَ.

وَلَا يَلْزَمُ مِنْ صِحَّةِ الكَرَامَةِ صِدْقُ مَنْ يَدَّعِيهَا بِدُونِ بَيِّنَةٍ أَوْ قَرَائِنَ جَلِيَّةٍ تُفِيدُ الجَزْمَ بِذَلِكَ وَإِنْ مَشَى عَلَى المَاءِ أَوْ طَارَ فِي الهَوَاءِ أَوْ سُخِّرَتْ لَهُ الجِنُّ وَالسِّبَاعُ حَتَّى نَنْظُرَ خَاتِمَتَهُ وَمُوَافَقَتَهُ لِلشَّرْعِ فِي الأَمْرِ وَالنَّهْيِ.

فَإِنْ وُجِدَ ذَلِكَ مِنْ جَاهِلٍ فَهُوَ مَخْرَقَةٌ وَمَكْرٌ مِنْ إِبْلِيسَ وَإِغْوَاءٌ وَإِضْلَالٌ.

وَلَا شَيْءَ عَلَى مَنْ ظَنَّ الخَيْرَ بِمَنْ رَآهُ مِنْهُ وَحُسْنُ الظَّنِّ بِأَهْلِ الدِّينِ حَسَنٌ.

أَفْضَلُ الخَلْقِ الأَنْبِيَاءُ عَلَيْهِمُ الصَّلَاةُ وَالسَّلَامُ

وَالأَنْبِيَاءُ أَفْضَلُ مِنَ الأَوْلِيَاءِ وَهُمَا أَفْضَلُ مِنَ المَلَائِكَةِ.

Types of Visions

Visions include that which is good. These are a portion of prophethood and are glad tidings seen by the believer and shown to them. They are words Allāh uses to communicate with the believer.

They also include muddled dreams, resulting from a mixture of things. They could be from the Shayṭān, his whispers, and nightmares; or from one's own consciousness, inspiration, or imagination.

Leadership

It is a legal obligation to install a leader. It is a public religious position which is a communal obligation.

It is an individual obligation only upon he who is worthy. Lots are drawn in the event there is more than one of the same caliber. There is absolutely nothing wrong if the superior leader becomes the lesser in merit.

Obligations of the Ruler

The ruler occupies the position of the Prophet of Quraysh ﷺ by establishing the religious law, supporting the truth and refuting falsehood, leading ḥajj, military campaigns, and the remaining acts of worship; establishing the penal code, ensuring justice for the oppressed, enjoining the good and forbidding the evil, protecting the community, championing public safety, maintaining unity, being aware of legal rulings, being of sound execution and management, being altruistic with righteousness, collecting the land-tax, spoils, and zakāt etc., and properly dispersing wealth along with anything else associated with him.

فِي أَنْوَاعِ الرُّؤْيَا

وَالرُّؤْيَا مِنْهَا الصَّالِحَةُ وَهِيَ جُزْءٌ مِن أَجْزَاءِ النُّبُوَّةِ وَهُوَ المُبَشِّرَاتُ يَرَاهَا المُؤْمِنَ وَتُرَى لَهُ وَهِيَ كَلَامٌ يُكَلِّمُهُ اللَّهُ لِلْمُؤْمِنِ. وَمِنْهَا أَضْغَاثُ أَحْلَامٍ وَ ثَمَرَةُ أَخْلَاطٍ وَمَا يَكُونُ مِنَ الشَّيْطَانِ وَوَسْوَاسِهِ وَتَحْزِينًا وَمِنْ حَدِيثِ النَّفْسِ وَإِلْهَامِهَا وَتَوَهُّمِهَا.

فِي الإِمَامَةِ

وَيَجِبُ إِقَامَةُ الإِمَامِ شَرْعًا وَهِيَ رُتْبَةٌ دِينِيَّةٌ عَامَّةٌ وَهِيَ فَرْضُ كِفَايَةٍ.

وَتَتَعَيَّنُ عَلَى مَنْ هُوَ أَهْلُهَا وَلَيْسَ غَيْرُهُ وَيُقْرَعُ مَعَ التَّسَاوِي وَإِنْ صَارَ الفَاضِلُ المُسْتَوْلِي مَفْضُولًا لَمْ يَضُرَّ مُطْلَقًا.

وَاجِبَاتُ إِمَامِ المُسْلِمِينَ

وَالإِمَامُ مَنْ قَامَ مَقَامَ النَّبِيِّ صَلَّى اللَّهُ عَلَيْهِ وَسَلَّمَ مِنْ قُرَيْشٍ فِي إِقَامَةِ قَانُونِ الشَّرْعِ مِنْ إِقَامَةِ الحَقِّ وَدَحْضِ البَاطِلِ وَالحَجِّ وَالغَزْوِ وَسَائِرِ العِبَادَاتِ وَإِقَامَةِ الحُدُودِ وَإِنْصَافِ المَظْلُومِ وَالأَمْرِ بِالمَعْرُوفِ وَالنَّهْيِ عَنِ المُنْكَرِ وَحِرَاسَةِ الأُمَّةِ وَحِمَايَةِ البَيْضَةِ وَجَمْعِ الكَلِمَةِ وَمَعْرِفَةِ الأَحْكَامِ وَصِحَّةِ التَّنْفِيذِ وَالتَّدْبِيرِ وَإِيثَارِ الطَّاعَةِ وَأَخْذِ الخَرَاجِ وَالفَيْءِ وَالزَّكَاةِ وَنَحْوِهَا وَصَرْفِ المَالِ فِي جِهَاتِهِ وَغَيْرِ ذَلِكَ مِنَ الأُمُورِ المُتَعَلِّقَةِ بِهِ.

Obeying the ruler in righteousness is an obligation and prohibited in sin. It is preferred when it comes to recommendations and abhorred when it comes to the disliked.

Leadership is established by way of appointment, interpretative judgement, selection, and sometimes by the dominance of a worthy party. It is solidified by agreement from the authorities who are upright and know who is appropriate, deserving, and more befitting for the position, more suitable than others for the people and the religion. The people of his region are like any other. It is not solidified for more than one.

Requirements of the Leader & Their Removal

It is stipulated that they be a Muslim of moral capacity, free and upright; with the ability to hear, see, and speak; knowledgeable of legal rulings, proficient in management, able to deliver rights to the deserving and all other matters pertaining to their position; male, brave, yielded to, effective, and from the tribe of Quraysh. If he proves to be incapable of fulfilling his obligations he is required to resign and if not, the people must remove him.

It is not permitted to revolt against them even if they be immoral. Rather, we are to pray behind them, make ḥajj with them, give them zakāt, the land tax, 10% tax etc., and pray for them.

If the pledge of allegiance is valid, no one can annul it.

Ranking the Companions

The best of mankind, after Allāh's messenger ﷺ, and most virtuous are Abū Bakr al-Ṣiddīq, the first caliph and leader, followed by ʿUmar b. al-Khaṭṭāb then ʿUthmān b. ʿAffān then ʿAlī b. Abī Ṭālib and then the remaining 10 including Ṭalḥah, al-Zubayr, Saʿd b. Abī Waqqāṣ, ʿAbd al-Raḥmān b. Aʿwf, Saʿīd b. Zayd b. ʿAmr b. Nufayl, and Abū ʿUbaydah b. al-Jarrāḥ.

وَتجِبُ طَاعَتهُ فِي الطَّاعَةِ وَتحْرُمُ فِي المَعْصِيَةِ وَتُسَنُّ فِي المَسْنُونِ وَتُكْرَه فِي المَكْرُوهِ.

وَتَثْبُتُ الإِمَامَةِ بِالنَّصِ وَالِاجْتِهَادِ وَالِاخْتِيَارِ أَوْبِالغَلَبَةِ تَارَةً مِمَّنْ يَصْلُحُ لَهَا. وَتَنْعَقِدُ بِاتِّفَاقِ أَهْلِ الحَلِّ وَالعَقْدِ عَلَيْهِ وَهُمْ عُدُولٌ يَعْرِفُونَ مَنْ يَصْلُحُ لَهَا وَيَسْتَحِقُّهَا وَأَوْلَى بِهَا وَأَصْلَحُ لِلنَّاسِ وَالدِّينِ مِنْ غَيْرِهِ وَأَهْلُ بَلَدِهِ كَغَيْرِهِمْ وَلَا تَنْعَقِدُ لِأَكْثَرَ مِنْ وَاحِدٍ.

شَرْطُ الإِمَامِ وَمَتَى يَعْزِلُ؟

وَشَرْطُهُ أَنْ يَكُونَ مُسْلِمًا مُكَلَّفًا حُرًّا عَدْلًا سَمِيعًا بَصِيرًا نَاطِقًا عَالِمًا بِأَحْكَامِ الشَّرْعِ خَبِيرًا بِتَدْبِيرِ الأُمُورِ قَادِرًا عَلَى إِيصَالِ الحَقِّ إِلَى مُسْتَحِقِّهِ وَعَلَى سَائِرِ مَا تَتَعَلَّقُ بِهِ ذَكَرًا شُجَاعًا مُطَاعَ الأَمْرِ نَافِذَ الحُكْمِ قُرَشِيًّا. فَإِنْ طَرَأَ لَهُ عَجْزٌ عَمَّا لَا بُدَّ مِنْهُ وَجَبَ عَلَيْهِ عَزْلَ نَفْسِهِ فَإِنْ أَبَى لَزِمَ النَّاسَ عَزْلُهُ.

وَلَا يَجُوزُ الخُرُوجَ عَلَيْهِ وَإِنْ كَانَ فَاسِقًا بَلْ نُصَلِّي خَلْفَهُ وَنَحُجُّ مَعَهُ وَنُعْطِيهِ الزَّكَاةَ وَالخَرَاجَ وَالعُشْرَ وَنَحْوَ ذَلِكَ وَنَدْعُو لَهُ. وَإِذَا صَحَّتْ البَيْعَةُ فَلَيْسَ لِأَحَدٍ فَسْخُهَا.

فِي المُفَاضَلَةِ بَيْنَ الصَّحَابَةِ

وَخَيْرُ النَّاسِ بَعْدَ رَسُولِ اللهِ صَلَّى اللهُ عَلَيْهِ وَسَلَّمَ وَأَفْضَلُهُمْ أَبُو بَكْرٍ الصِّدِّيقُ وَهُوَ أَوَّلُ الخُلَفَاءِ وَالأَئِمَةِ ثُمَّ عُمَرُ بْنُ الخَطَّابِ ثُمَّ عُثْمَانُ ثُمَّ عَلِيّ بْنُ أَبِي طَالِبٍ ثُمَّ بَقِيَّةُ العَشَرَةِ وَهُمْ طَلْحَةُ وَالزُّبَيْرُ وَسَعْدُ بْنُ أَبِي وَقَّاصٍ وَعَبْدُالرَّحْمَنِ بْنُ عَوْفٍ وَسَعِيدُ بْنُ زَيْدِ بْنِ عَمْرِو بْنِ نُفَيْلٍ وَأَبُو عُبَيْدَةَ ابْنُ الجَرَّاحِ.

In subsequent virtue are the people of Badr from the muhājirūn and then the Anṣār, in subsequent order according to their migration followed by the remaining companions of Allāh's messenger, who all have a rank, and then the following generation, followed by their followers in righteousness, and then Allāh knows best.

The Most Virtuous Women

ʿĀ'ishah, may Allāh be pleased with her, is the most virtuous woman followed by Khadijah and then Fāṭimah.

The Muslim's Obligation Regarding the Companions

It obligatory to love all the companions and to abstain from what occurred between them by way of writing, reading, listening, and telling others. It is obligatory to mention their good qualities, pray that Allāh is pleased with them, refrain from harboring any bias against them, and to have conviction in affording them excuse as they did what they did based on acceptable reasoning which will result in their reward; those who were correct will have two rewards and those who erred will have one.

Those Who Curse the Companions

Whoever curses one of them, deeming it to be permissible, has disbelieved; otherwise, they are considered immoral (categorical disbelief has been narrated). If they deem them immoral or speak evil of their religiosity, they have disbelieved. Whoever ranks ʿAlī above Abū Bakr or ʿUmar or gives him preference is virtue and leadership, apart from lineage, is an immoral rāfiḍī innovator, but not a disbeliever. If they deny Abū Bakr's companionship, slander ʿĀ'ishah, or believe that Jibrīl erred regarding the revelation, they have disbelieved.

ثُمَّ بَعْدَهُمْ فِي الفَضْلِ أَهْلُ بَدْرٍ المُهَاجِرِينَ ثُمَّ الأَنْصَارُ عَلَى قَدْرِ الهِجْرَةِ أَوَّلًا فَأَوَّلًا ثُمَّ سَائِرُ أَصْحَابِ رَسُولِ اللَّهِ صَلَّى اللَّهُ عَلَيْهِ وَسَلَّمَ وَلَهُمْ رُتَبٌ رَضِيَ اللَّهُ تَعَالَى عَنْهُمْ ثُمَّ التَّابِعُونَ ثُمَّ تَابِعُوهُمْ بِإِحْسَانٍ ثُمَّ اللَّهُ أَعْلَمُ.

أَفْضَلُ النِّسَاءِ

وَعَائِشَةُ رَضِيَ اللَّهُ تَعَالَى عَنْهَا أَفْضَلُ النِّسَاءِ ثُمَّ خَدِيجَةُ ثُمَّ فَاطِمَةُ.

مَا يَجِبُ لِلصَّحَابَةِ عَلَى المُسْلِمِينَ

وَيَجِبُ حُبُّ كُلِّ الصَّحَابَةِ وَالكَفُّ عَمَّا جَرَى بَيْنَهُمْ كِتَابَةً وَقِرَاءَةً وَسَمَاعًا وَتَسْمِيعًا. وَيَجِبُ ذِكْرُ مَحَاسِنِهِمْ وَالتَّرَاضِي عَنْهُمْ وَتَرْكُ التَّحَامُلِ عَلَيْهِمْ وَاعْتِقَادُ العُذْرِ لَهُمْ لِأَنَّهُمْ إِنَّمَا فَعَلُوا مَا فَعَلُوا بِاجْتِهَادٍ سَائِغٍ يُثَابُونَ عَلَيْهِ فَلِمُصِيبِهِمْ أَجْرَانِ وَلِمُخْطِئِهِمْ أَجْرٌ وَاحِدٌ.

حُكْمُ سَابِّ الصَّحَابَةِ

فَمَنْ سَبَّ أَحَدًا مِنْهُمْ مُسْتَحِلًّا كَفَرَ وَإِنْ لَمْ يَسْتَحِلَّ فَسَقَ وَعَنْهُ يَكْفُرُ مُطْلَقًا وَإِنْ فَسَّقَهُمْ أَوْ طَعَنَ فِي دِينِهِمْ كَفَرَ. وَمَنْ فَضَّلَ عَلِيًّا عَلَى أَبِي بَكْرٍ أَوْ عُمَرَ أَوْ قَدَّمَهُ عَلَيْهِمَا فِي الفَضِيلَةِ وَالإِمَامَةِ دُونَ النَّسَبِ فَهُوَ رَافِضِيٌّ وَمُبْتَدِعٌ فَاسِقٌ غَيْرُ كَافِرٍ.

وَإِنْ أَنْكَرَ صُحْبَةَ أَبِي بَكْرٍ أَوْ قَذَفَ عَائِشَةَ أَوْ اعْتَقَدَ أَنَّ جِبْرِيلَ غَلِطَ فِي الوَحْيِ كَفَرَ.

Rules Regarding Enjoining the Good & Forbidding the Evil

Enjoining the Good and Forbidding the Evil is a communal obligation upon the community and an individual obligation upon someone who is all alone. It is an obligation upon the one who knows it, clearly understands it, and has witnessed it; knows what is being forbidden; is not afraid of the whip or cane; being harmed physically or financially; harm befalling one's family, or turmoil arising greater than the evil; and knows that it will be effective while no one else will do it, and if not, then it is permissible even if harm is feared.

The head of state and ruler are the same regarding the ruling as are the scholar and the layman, upright and the immoral.

The best form is done by the hand, then the tongue, and the weakest is in the heart which is an individual obligation that is not voided under any circumstance.

The public is obliged to help those forbidding and support them according to their ability. They are not to forbid with the sword or the cane without the authorities.

As for someone who adheres to a school of thought, they are reproached for opposing it if they have no substantial evidence, acceptable precedent, or obvious excuse.

Al-mʿarūf is every good statement, action, or intent as defined by the law. Al-munkar is every evil statement, action, or intent as defined by the law.

It is obligatory to reproach one for abandoning an obligation or engaging in the impermissible. As for things that are either preferred or disliked, it is preferred.

فِي أَحْكَامِ الأَمْرِ بِالمَعْرُوفِ وَالنَّهْيِ عَنِ المُنْكَرِ

الأَمْرُ بِالمَعْرُوفِ وَالنَّهْيُ عَنْ المنْكَرِ فَرْضُ كِفَايَةٍ عَلَى الجَمَاعَةِ وَعَيْنٌ عَلَى الوَاحِدِ.

فَيَجِبُ عَلَى مَنْ عَلِمَهُ وَتَحَقَّقَهُ وَشَاهَدَ وَهُوَ عَارِفٌ بِمَا يُنْكِرُهُ وَلَمْ يَخَفْ سَوْطًا وَلَا عَصًا وَلَا أَذًى فِي نَفْسِهِ أَوْ مَالِهِ أَوْ أَهْلِهِ وَلَا فِتْنَةً تَزِيدُ عَلَى المُنْكَرِ إِذَا عَلِمَ حُصُولَ المَقْصُودِ بِهِ وَلَمْ يَقُمْ بِهِ غَيْرُهُ وَإِلَّا جَازَ وَإِنْ خَافَ أَذًى.

وَسَوَاءٌ فِي ذَلِكَ الإِمَامُ وَالحَاكِمُ وَالعَالِمُ وَالجَاهِلُ وَالعَدْلُ وَالفَاسِقُ.

وَأَعْلَاهُ بِاليَدِ ثُمَّ بِاللِّسَانِ وَأَضْعَفُهُ بِالقَلْبِ وَهُوَ بِهِ فَرْضُ عَيْنٍ وَلَا يَسْقُطُ بِحَالٍ.

وَعَلَى النَّاسِ إِعَانَةُ المُنْكِرِ وَنَصْرُهُ مَعَ القُدْرَةِ وَلَا يُنْكِرُ بِسَيْفٍ وَلَا عَصًا إِلَّا مَعَ سُلْطَانٍ.

وَمَنْ الْتَزَمَ مَذْهَبًا أُنْكِرَ عَلَيْهِ مُخَالَفَتُهُ بِلَا دَلِيلٍ ثَابِتٍ أَوْ تَقْلِيدٍ سَائِغٍ أَوْ عُذْرٍ ظَاهِرٍ.

وَالمَعْرُوفُ كُلُّ قَوْلٍ وَفِعْلٍ وَقَصْدٍ حَسَنٍ شَرْعًا وَالمُنْكَرُ كُلُّ قَوْلٍ وَفِعْلٍ وَقَصْدٍ قُبِحَ شَرْعًا.

وَالإِنْكَارُ فِي تَرْكِ الوَاجِبِ وَفِعْلِ الحَرَامِ وَاجِبٌ وَفِي تَرْكِ المَنْدُوبِ وَعَدَمِ تَعَلُّمِهِ وَتَعْلِيمِهِ وَفِي فِعْلِ المَكْرُوهِ وَتَعَلُّمِهِ وَتَعْلِيمِهِ مَنْدُوبٌ.

Rights Regarding What is Being Joined & Forbidden

Everything which is commanded or forbidden falls within three categories; the rights of Allāh, like prayer, fasting, encouragement to do good and leave evil.

The rights of mankind like injustice or oppression, etc.

Or a combination of the two like zakat, expiations, the penalty for slander etc.

And therefore, all are equal when approached be they a father or anyone else.

Qualities of Those Who Enjoin the Good & Forbid the Evil

Those who enjoin the good and forbid the evil should be humble and gentle when inviting others, compassionate and merciful, not hardhearted, overly stern, or unyielding; free and fair, knowledgeable of what it is they are enjoining or forbidding; pious, virtuous, and chaste; of sound counsel, aware of Allāh's supervision, and deeply religious.

It should be done sincerely for Allāh to establish the faith and aid the law in accordance with His order while enlivening the practice of the Prophet ﷺ. There should be no adulation, hypocrisy, or flattery. It should not be done in competition with others or to boast. It should not be from someone whose words contradict their actions.

It is however an obligation to reproach the sinner even if the one reproaching is a partner in that sin to avoid two sins. What was mentioned previously is considered the best qualities.

It is preferred to perform voluntary deeds, be compassionate, smile, display good manners when reproaching, to be resolute, and to be forgiving with lapses a time or two.

الحُقُوق فِيمَا يُؤْمَرُ بِهِ وَيُنْهَى عَنْهُ ثَلَاثَةٌ

وَكُلُّ مَا يُؤْمَرُ بِهِ وَيُنْهَى فَإِمَّا حَقُّ اللَّهِ تَعَالَى كَالصَّلَاةِ وَالصَّومِ وَالحَثِّ عَلَى الطَّاعَةِ وَتَرْكِ المَعْصِيَةِ.

أَوْ لِآدَمِيٍّ كَالمَطْلِ بِالمَالِ وَالحَيْفِ وَالظُّلْمِ وَنَحْوِ ذَلِكَ.

أَوْ لَهُمَا كَالزَّكَاةِ وَالكَفَّارَةِ وَحَدِّ القَذْفِ وَنَحْوِ ذَلِكَ.

وَالأَبُ وَغَيْرُهُ فِي الإِنْكَارِ عَلَيْهِ سَوَاءٌ.

صِفَاتُ الآمِرِ بِالمَعْرُوفِ وَالنَّاهِي عَنْ المُنْكَرِ

يَنْبَغِي أَنْ يَكُونَ الآمِرُ بِالمَعْرُوفِ وَالنَّاهِي عَنِ المُنْكَرِ مُتَوَاضِعًا رَفِيقًا فِيمَا يَدْعُو إِلَيْهِ شَفِيقًا رَحِيمًا غَيْرَ فَظٍّ وَلَا غَلِيظَ القَلْبِ وَلَا مُتَعَنِّتٍ حُرًّا عَدْلًا فَقِيهًا عَالِمًا بِالمَأْمُورَاتِ وَالمَنْهِيَاتِ شَرْعًا. دَيِّنًا نَزِهًا عَفِيفًا ذَا رَأْيٍ وَمُرَاقَبَةٍ وَشِدَّةٍ فِي الدِّينِ.

قَاصِدًا بِذَلِكَ وَجْهَ اللَّهِ تَعَالَى وَإِقَامَةَ دِينِهِ وَنُصْرَةَ شَرْعِهِ وَامْتِثَالَ أَمْرِهِ وَإِحْيَاءَ سُنَّةِ نَبِيِّهِ بِلَا رِيَاءٍ وَلَا مُنَافَقَةٍ وَلَا مُدَاهَمَةٍ غَيْرَ مُنَافِسٍ وَلَا مُفَاخِرٍ وَلَا مِمَّنْ يُخَالِفُ قَوْلُهُ فِعْلَهُ.

لَكِنْ يَجِبُ عَلَيْهِ الإِنْكَارُ وَإِنْ كَانَ شَرِيكًا فِي المَعْصِيَةِ لِئَلَا يَجْمَعَ بَيْنَ مَعْصِيَتَيْنِ فَمَا ذُكِرَ مُعْتَبَرٌ لِلْأَكْمَلِ. وَتُسَنُّ العَمَلُ بِالنَّوَافِلِ وَالرِّفْقُ وَطَلَاقَةُ الوَجْهِ وَحُسْنُ الخُلُقِ عِنْدَ إِنْكَارِهِ وَالتَّثَبُّتُ وَالمُسَامَحَةُ بِالهَفْوَةِ مَرَّةً وَمَرَّتَيْنِ.

Gradualism in Forbidding & Abandoning the Sinner

The process begins with that which is easiest and gradually increases if it does not desist. If it then does not desist, it should be brought to the attention of the just authorities; money is not to be taken nor anything done beyond what is obligatory. The ruler/authorities is reproached by way of fair preaching and spiritual incitement.

It is recommended to abandon the sinners who publicize their sins. It is a must to look past those who conceal their sins though they should be advised in private.

It is impermissible to challenge an evil committed far away, to uncover someone concealed or to divulge them, particularly with evidence.

Abandoning the innovator who invites others to misguidance is obligatory upon anyone who cannot bring about rectification and rebuke them, or who is not safe from their influence.

Rules to Defending One's Rights

It is an obligation upon the capable to defend themselves and their honor and it is permissible to defend their wealth.

It is required to defend a fellow Muslim along with their wealth and honor if possible. It is however voided if it is known that there is no benefit.

Also, saving them from drowning and burning etc. just like starvation if they have the ability.

التَّدَرُّجُ فِي النَّهْيِ وَهِجْرَانُ العُصَاةِ

وَيَبْدَأُ فِي إِنْكَارِهِ بِالأَسْهَلِ فَالأَسْهَلُ فَإِنْ زَالَ وَإِلَّا زَادَ فَإِنْ لَمْ يَزَلْ رَفَعَهُ إِلَى سُلْطَانٍ عَادِلٍ لَا يَأْخُذُ مَالًا وَلَا يَفْعَلُ غَيْرَ مَا يَجِبُ وَيُنْكِرُ عَلَى السُّلْطَانِ بِالوَعْظِ وَالتَّخْوِيفِ.

وَيُسَنُّ هِجْرَانُ العُصَاةِ المُتَظَاهِرِينَ بِالمَعْصِيَةِ وَيَجِبُ الإِغْضَاءُ عَنِ المُسْتَتِرِينَ الكَاتِمِينَ لَهَا لَكِنْ يَنْبَغِي نُصْحُهُمْ سِرًّا.

وَيَحْرُمُ التَّعَرُّضُ لِمُنْكَرٍ فُعِلَ بَعِيدًا وَكَشْفُ مَسْتُورٍ وَإِشَاعَتُهُ وَتَتَبُّعُهُ لَا سِيَّمَا بِالبَيِّنَةِ.

وَيَجِبُ هِجْرَانُ المُبْتَدِعِينَ الدَّاعِينَ إِلَى الضَّلَالَةِ عَلَى مَنْ عَجَزَ عَنْ إِصْلَاحِهِمْ وَالإِنْكَارُ عَلَيْهِمْ أَوْ لَمْ يَأْمَنِ الاغْتِرَارَ بِهِمْ.

فِي أَحْكَامِ دَفْعِ الصَّائِلِ

وَيَجِبُ عَلَى القَادِرِ الدَّفْعُ عَنْ نَفْسِهِ وَحُرْمَتِهِ وَيَجُوزُ عَنْ مَالِهِ.

وَيَلْزَمُهُ الدَّفْعُ عَنْ أَخِيهِ المُسْلِمِ وَمَالِهِ وَحُرْمَتِهِ إِنْ أَمْكَنَهُ وَيَسْقُطُ إِنْ عَلِمَ أَنَّهُ لَا يُفِيدُ.

وَعَلَيْهِ إِنْجَاؤُهُ مِنْ غَرَقٍ وَحَرِيقٍ وَنَحْوِهِمَا كَالمَجَاعَةِ مَعَ القُدْرَةِ.

Epilogue

Obligations & Blind Following

Obligations are of two types: individual obligations and communal obligations. Individual obligations include that without which Islām would not be complete, one of its pillars, or a prerequisite. All else are communal obligations.

The categories of both liked and disliked could include everyone and could be specific. Whatever is required to fulfill an obligation is too an obligation.

Blind following and following speculation is not allowed for anything which requires resolution as it is does not result in it.

Things which require resolution are only sufficed with definitive evidence. Things which do not require resolution, only speculation, permit blind following which is substantiated by speculative evidence.

Definitive Evidence

Definitive evidence is either purely intellectual e.g. like saying each in a pair is a consort, each consort has half, therefore each in a pair has a half, and like absolute induction which is a general ruling based on the ruling of its specifics; or purely legal such as the Book, mutawātir Sunnah, and consensus if founded upon evidence and mass transmission.

Whatever has been reported of the Sunnah or consensus via singular transmission which results in resolution with either verbal or contextual support is just like that which has been mass transmitted, otherwise it is not.

Or it is a synthesis of the two like when we say every inebriant is an intoxicant and every intoxicant is impermissible and therefore every inebriant is impermissible.

الخَاتِمَةُ

فِي أَقْسَامِ الفَرْضِ وَمَتَى يَمْتَنِـعُ التَّقْلِيدُ وَمَتَى يَجُوزُ

وَالفَرْضُ قِسْمَانِ فَرْضُ عَيْنٍ وَفَرْضُ كِفَايَةٍ فَمَا لَا يَتِمُّ الإِسْلَامُ بِدُونِهِ أَوْ هُوَ رُكْنٌ فِيهِ أَوْ شَرْطٌ فَرْضُ عَيْنٍ وَمَا عَدَا ذَلِكَ فَرْضُ كِفَايَةٍ.

وَالمَنْدُوبُ وَالمَكْرُوهُ قَدْ يَعُمَّانِ الأَعْيَانَ وَقَدْ يَخُصَّانِ وَمَا لَا يَتِمُّ الوَاجِبُ إِلَّا بِهِ فَهُوَ وَاجِبٌ.

وَكُلُّ مَا يُطْلَبُ فِيهِ الجَزْمُ يَمْتَنِـعُ التَّقْلِيدُ فِيهِ وَالأَخْذُ فِيهِ بِالظَّنِّ لِأَنَّهُ لَا يُفِيدُهُ.

وَكُلُّ مَطْلُوبٍ جَازِمٍ إِنَّمَا يُفِيدُهُ دَلِيلٌ قَطْعِيٌّ وَكُلُّ مَا لَا يُطْلَبُ فِيهِ الجَزْمُ بَلِ الظَّنُّ يَجُوزُ التَّقْلِيدُ فِيهِ وَإِثْبَاتُهُ بِدَلِيلٍ ظَنِّيٍّ.

فِي أَقْسَامِ الدَّلِيلِ القَطْعِيِّ

وَالدَّلِيلُ القَطْعِيُّ إِمَّا عَقْلِيٌّ مَحْضٌ كَقَوْلِنَا كُلُّ اثْنَيْنِ زَوْجٌ وَكُلُّ زَوْجٍ لَهُ نِصْفٌ فَكُلُّ اثْنَيْنِ لَهُمَا نِصْفٌ وَكَالاِسْتِقْرَاءِ التَّامِّ وَهُوَ الحُكْمُ عَلَى الكُلِّيِّ بِمَا حُكِمَ بِهِ عَلَى جُزْئِيَّاتِهِ.

وَإِمَّا شَرْعِيٌّ مَحْضٌ كَالكِتَابِ وَالسُّنَّةِ المُتَوَاتِرَةِ وَإِجْمَاعِ الأُمَّةِ إِذَا نَصَبُوا عَلَيْهِ دَلِيلًا وَنُقِلَ مُتَوَاتِرًا.

وَمَا نُقِلَ آحَادًا مِنَ السُّنَّةِ وَالإِجْمَاعِ وَأَفَادَ الجَزْمَ مَعَ قَرَائِنَ قَوْلِيَّةٍ أَوْ حَالِيَّةٍ فَهُوَ كَالمُتَوَاتِرِ وَإِلَّا فَلَا.

وَإِمَّا مُرَكَّبٌ مِنْهُمَا كَقَوْلِنَا كُلُّ مُسْكِرٍ خَمْرٌ وَكُلُّ خَمْرٍ حَرَامٌ فَكُلُّ مُسْكِرٍ حَرَامٌ.

Speculative evidence is like what is apparent from the Book and Sunnah, apparent consensus, a companion's juristic school, a previous legislation etc. This introduction does not have the capacity for a more comprehensive presentation on evidence in general, so whoever would like additional information should refer to more lengthy works.

Those Who Oppose Definitive Evidence

Whoever opposes the result of definitive evidence, which is something indispensable of Islām, has disbelieved; if it is not, they have strayed.

Declaring Apostasy, Immorality, & Cursing Disbelievers

Whoever declares, with conviction, another to be a disbeliever who is not a disbeliever has themselves disbelieved. Whoever declares, with conviction, another to be immoral who is not immoral is themselves immoral.

It is impermissible to curse a specific disbeliever.

Theological Terms

Kullu Mawjūdin Ḥaqīqatan: Everything which results in a proven reality which is perceived both in the mind or with the senses. Denying it is misguidance.

Al-Jawhar: That which occupies space, is independently existent, has several attributes, and cannot be divided.

Al-ʿAraḍ: That which is dependent on another for occupancy and attribution.

Al-Jism: That which comprises two or more parts.

وَالظَّنِّيُّ كَظَاهِرِ الكِتَابِ وَالسُّنَّةِ وَكَظَاهِرِ الإِجْمَاعِ وَكَمَذْهَبِ الصَّحَابِيِّ وَشَرْعِ مَنْ قَبْلَنَا وَغَيْرِ ذَلِكَ وَتَمَامُ القَوْلِ فِي الدَّلِيلِ مُطْلَقًا لَا تَحْتَمِلُهُ هَذِهِ المُقَدِّمَةُ فَمَنْ رَامَ أَكْثَرَ مِنْ ذَلِكَ فَعَلَيْهِ بِالمُطَوَّلَاتِ.

فِي حُكْمِ مَنْ خَالَفَ مُوجِبَ دَلِيلٍ قَطْعِيٍّ

وَمَنْ خَالَفَ مُوجِبَ دَلِيلٍ قَطْعِيٍّ كَفَرَ إِنْ كَانَ مِمَّا لَا يَتِمُّ الإِسْلَامُ بِدُونِهِ وَإِلَّا فَسَقَ.

حُكْمُ التَّكْفِيرِ وَالتَّفْسِيقِ وَحُكْمُ لَعْنِ كَافِرٍ مُعَيَّنٍ

وَمَنْ كَفَّرَ مَنْ لَيْسَ بِكَافِرٍ مُعْتَقِدًا كُفْرَهُ كَفَرَ وَمَنْ فَسَّقَ مَنْ لَيْسَ بِفَاسِقٍ مُعْتَقِدًا فِسْقَهُ فَسَقَ.

وَيَحْرُمُ لَعْنُ كَافِرٍ مُعَيَّنٍ.

فِي تَعْرِيفِ بَعْضِ الاِصْطِلَاحَاتِ الكَلَامِيَّةِ

وَكُلُّ مَوْجُودٍ حَقِيقَةٌ هُوَ كُلُّ مُؤَدٍّ إِلَى حَقِيقَةٍ ثَابِتَةٍ تُعْلَمُ عَقْلًا أَوْ حِسًّا فَإِنْكَارُهُ سَفْسَطَةٌ.

وَالجَوْهَرُ مَا شَغَلَ حَيِّزًا وَقَامَ بِنَفْسِهِ وَحَمَلَ بَعْضَ الأَعْرَاضِ وَلَمْ يَقْبَلِ انْقِسَامًا.

وَالعَرَضُ مَا افْتَقَرَ إِلَى مَحَلٍّ يَقُومُ بِهِ يَحْمِلُهُ.

الجِسْمُ مَا تَأَلَّفَ مِنْ جُزْأَيْنِ فَصَاعِدًا.

Al-Qadīm: That which has not beginning to its existence and is not preceded by absence. It could also mean that which has preceded even if absence preceded it.

Al-Muḥdath: That which has a beginning to it existence and was preceded by absence. It could also mean that of which its existence succeeded something else.

Al-ʿĀlam: Every existent besides Allāh the Most High and His attributes.

Al-Mustaḥīl li-dhāti: This which is neither possible nor decreed otherwise it becomes possible.

Al-Jāʾiz: Whatever's convention or adjournment could be sensed or imagined. Legally it means whatever has been permitted by the law.

Al-Mumkin: Whatever's occurrence could be sensed, imagined, or legally allowed.

Al-Dawr: each of two things preceding the other which is false. Tasalsul is the same which is to arrange things in a perpetual order.

Categories of Combined Givens

Combined givens are:

Naqīḍān: two things which can neither exist together nor be absent at the same time.

Khilāfān: two things which can exist together and be absent at the same time.

Ḍiddān: two things which cannot exist together but can be absent at the same time due to their different realities.

Mithlān: two things which cannot exist together but can be absent at the same time due to their equal realities.

The realities of every combined thing is as follows.

وَالقَدِيمُ مَا لَا أَوَّلَ لِوُجُودِهِ وَلَمْ يَسْبِقْهُ عَدَمٌ وَقَدْ يُرَادُ بِهِ المُتَقَدِّمُ وَإِنْ سَبَقَهُ العَدَمُ.

وَالمُحْدَثُ مَا لِوُجُودِهِ أَوَّلٌ وَيَسْبِقُهُ العَدَمُ وَقَدْ يُرَادُ بِهِ مَا تَأَخَّرَ وُجُودُهُ عَنْ شَيْءٍ آخَرَ.

وَالعَالَمُ كُلُّ مَوجُودٍ سِوَى اللهِ تَعَالَى وَصِفَاتِهِ.

وَالمُسْتَحِيلُ لِذَاتِهِ غَيْرُ مُمْكِنٍ وَلَا مَقْدُورٍ وَإِلَّا صَارَ مُمْكِنًا.

وَالجَائِزُ مَا جَازَ اجْتِمَاعُهُ وَافْتِرَاقُهُ حِسًّا أَوْ وَهْمًا وَهُوَ شَرْعًا مَا أُذِنَ فِي الشَّرْعِ.

وَالمُمْكِنُ مَا جَازَ وُقُوعُهُ حِسًّا أَوْ وَهْمًا أَوْ شَرْعًا.

وَالدَّوْرُ بِمَعْنَى تَقَدُّمِ كُلٍّ مِنْ شَيْئَيْنِ عَلَى الآخَرِ بَاطِلٌ وَكَذَلِكَ التَّسَلْسُلُ وَهُوَ تَرَتُّبُ أُمُورٍ غَيْرِ مُتَنَاهِيَةٍ.

فِي أَقْسَامِ المَعْلُومَيْنِ

المَعْلُومَيْنِ

إِمَّا نَقِيضَانِ لَا يَرْتَفِعَانِ وَلَا يَجْتَمِعَانِ.

أَوْ خِلَافَانِ يَجْتَمِعَانِ وَيَرْتَفِعَانِ.

أَوْ ضِدَّانِ لَا يَجْتَمِعَانِ وَيَرْتَفِعَانِ لِاخْتِلَافِ الحَقِيقَةِ.

أَوْ مِثْلَانِ لَا يَجْتَمِعَانِ وَيَرْتَفِعَانِ لِتَسَاوِي الحَقِيقَةِ.

وَكُلُّ شَيْئَيْنِ حَقِيقَتَاهُمَا

They are equal and therefore the presence of each requires the presence of the other and vice versa.

They are different and therefore they do not share the same occupancy, one is absolutely more general and the other is absolutely more specific and so one is found in the presence of every entity of the other but not vice versa, or one is more general in a sense and the other more specific in a sense and therefore they are found together and with others.

Definition of Technical Terms

Al-ʿIlm: A quality by which its possessor is decisively distinguished in an accurate manner.

Al-Ẓann: the preponderance of one view over all others, the legitimacy of which is believed to be highly unlikely. If it is accurate then it is correct but if not, it is compound ignorance.

Al-Naẓar: The arrangement of premises in a manner which yields the desired outcome. It is either absolute or not. Both of which are either accurate or not. That which is accurate is correct, otherwise it is wrong.

Its prerequisites are reason, absence of that which is contrary to al-ʿIlm, and the absence of doubt.

Reason is the tool of discernment and is a natural aptitude and like some types of instinctual knowledge, is not acquired but created by Allāh the Most-High to distinguish between man and beast, prepare them to received knowledge, and manage complex thought. It is as if it is a light placed in the heart just like instinctual knowledge of what is necessary, possible, and absurd. Puerility and the like veil it. It is of varying degrees and can increase. Its location is the heart and it has a connection with the brain.

إِمَّا مُتَسَاوِيَتَانِ يَلْزَمُ مِنْ وُجُودِ كُلٍّ وُجُودُ الآخَرِ وَعَكْسُهُ.

أَوْ مُتَبَايِنَتَانِ لَا يَجْتَمِعَانِ فِي مَحَلٍّ وَاحِدٍ.

أَوْ إِحْدَاهُمَا أَعَمُّ مُطْلَقًا وَالأُخْرَى أَخَصُّ مُطْلَقًا تُوجَدُ إِحْدَاهُمَا مَعَ وُجُودِ كُلِّ أَفْرَادِ الأُخْرَى بِلَا عَكْسٍ. أَوْ إِحْدَاهُمَا أَعَمُّ مِنْ وَجْهٍ وَالأُخْرَى أَخَصُّ مِنْ وَجْهٍ تُوجَدُ كُلٌّ مَعَ الأُخْرَى وَبِدُونِهَا.

فِي تَعْرِيفِ الْعِلْمِ وَالظَّنِّ وَالنَّظَرِ وَالْعَقْلِ

الْعِلْمُ صِفَةٌ يُمَيِّزُ الْمُتَّصِفُ بِهَا تَمْيِيزًا جَازِمًا مُطَابِقًا لِمَا فِي نَفْسِ الأَمْرِ.

وَالظَّنُّ رُجْحَانُ اعْتِقَادٍ عَلَى غَيْرِهِ فِي نَفْسِ الْمُعْتَقِدِ مَعَ تَجْوِيزِهِ لِذَلِكَ الْغَيْرِ عَلَى بُعْدٍ فَإِنْ طَابَقَ فَصَادِقٌ وَإِلَّا فَجَهْلٌ مُرَكَّبٌ.

وَالنَّظَرُ تَرْتِيبُ مُقَدِّمَاتٍ تَرْتِيبًا مُوصِلًا إِلَى الْمَطْلُوبِ وَهُوَ إِمَّا جَازِمٌ أَوْ لَا وَكُلٌّ مِنْهُمَا إِمَّا مُطَابِقٌ أَوْ لَا فَالْمُطَابِقُ صَحِيحٌ وَغَيْرُهُ فَاسِدٌ.

وَشَرْطُهُ الْعَقْلُ وَانْتِفَاءُ ضِدِّ الْعِلْمِ وَعَدَمُ الشُّبْهَةِ.

وَالْعَقْلُ مَا يَحْصُلُ بِهِ الْمَيْزُ وَهُوَ غَرِيزَةٌ وَبَعْضُ الْعُلُومِ الضَّرُورِيَّةِ وَلَيْسَ مُكْتَسَبًا بَلْ خَلَقَهُ اللَّهُ تَعَالَى. يُفَارِقُ بِهِ الإِنْسَانُ الْبَهِيمَةَ وَيَسْتَعِدُّ بِهِ لِقَبُولِ الْعِلْمِ وَتَدْبِيرِ الصَّنَائِعِ الْفِكْرِيَّةِ فَكَأَنَّهُ نُورٌ يُقْذَفُ فِي الْقَلْبِ كَالْعِلْمِ الضَّرُورِيِّ بِالْوَاجِدِ وَالْمُمْكِنِ وَالْمُمْتَنِعِ.

وَالصِّبَا وَنَحْوُهُ حِجَابٌ لَهُ وَهُوَ مُتَفَاوِتٌ وَيَزِيدُ. وَمَحَلُّهُ الْقَلْبُ وَلَهُ اتِّصَالٌ بِالدِّمَاغِ.

Surrender is the Safe Way

The safest way is surrender. The faith of whoever does not surrender to Allāh and His messenger and leave that which is ambiguous to the one who knows, is not safe. Whoever seeks to know that which is impossible to comprehend and is not satisfied with submission, their aspiration will veil them from pure monotheism, unadulterated gnosis, and genuine faith.

They will waver between affirmation and denial; be riddled with anxiety, erratic, doubtful, divergent, confused, and perplexed; they will not be a sincere believer, a disavowing denier, or a certain inquisitor.

Whoever does not avoid negation and comparison has strayed and will not actualize de-anthropomorphism.

Penetrating deep into thought is the means of failure, the stairway to deprivation, the threshold of oppression, and is the stuff of misguidance and bewilderment. It typically opens the door to confusion and is rare that it is not accompanied by disappointment, delusion, estrangement, and anger with and avoidance of the Muslim community.

Feelings of assurance and despair are what removes one from the religion. For the people of the qiblah, the way to truth is between the two; between excessiveness and negligence, comparison and denial, and between compulsion and free-will.

The Author's Advice & Parting Counsel

Adhere to following: the people of prophetic tradition and narration without the people of ideation and innovation for even a little of that coupled with acumen is an abundance and a lot coupled with stupidity is only slightly harmful.

التَّسْلِيمُ أَسْلَمُ الطُّرقِ

أَسْلَمُ الطُّرُقِ التَّسْلِيمُ فَمَا سَلِمَ دِينُ مَنْ لَمْ يُسْلِمْ لِلَّهِ وَلِرَسُولِهِ وَرَدَّ عِلْمَ مَا اشْتَبَهَ إِلَى عَالِمِهِ وَمَنْ أَرَادَ عِلْمَ مَا يَمْتَنِعُ عِلْمُهُ وَلَمْ يَقْنَعْ بِالتَّسْلِيمِ حَجَبَهُ مَرَامُهُ عَنْ خَالِصِ التَّوْحِيدِ وَصَافِي المَعْرِفَةِ وَصَحِيحِ الإِيمَانِ.

فَيَتَرَدَّدُ بَيْنَ الإِقْرَارِ وَالإِنْكَارِ مُوَسْوِسًا تَائِهًا شَاكًّا زَائِغًا مُحَيَّرًا وَالِهًا لَا مُؤْمِنًا مُصَدِّقًا وَلَا جَاحِدًا مُكَذِّبًا وَلَا مُوقِنًا مُحَقِّقًا.

وَمَنْ لَمْ يَتَوَقَّ النَّفْيَ وَالتَّشْبِيهَ ضَلَّ وَلَمْ يُصِبِ التَّنْزِيهَ.

وَالتَّعَمُّقُ فِي الفِكْرِ ذَرِيعَةُ الخِذْلَانِ وَسُلَّمُ الحِرْمَانِ وَدَرَجَةُ الطُّغْيَانِ وَمَادَّةُ التَّوَهَانِ وَالوَلَهَانِ فَإِنَّهُ يَفْتَحُ بَابَ الحَيْرَةِ غَالِبًا وَقَلَّ أَنْ يَكُونَ مُلَازِمُهُ إِلَّا خَائِبًا وَلِلْوَهْمِ جَالِبًا وَلِلْبُعْدِ طَالِبًا وَلِلْأُمَّةِ مُجَانِبًا وَمُغَاضِبًا.

وَالأَمْنُ وَاليَأْسُ يَنْقُلَانِ عَنِ المِلَّةِ وَسَبِيلُ الحَقِّ بَيْنَهُمَا لِأَهْلِ القِبْلَةِ فَإِنَّهُ بَيْنَ الغُلُوِّ وَالتَّقْصِيرِ وَالتَّشْبِيهِ وَالتَّعْطِيلِ وَبَيْنَ الجَبْرِ وَالقَدَرِ.

نَصِيحَةُ المُؤَلِّفِ وَوَصِيَّتُهُ

فَعَلَيْكَ يَا أَخِي بِاتِّبَاعِ أَهْلِ السُّنَّةِ وَالآثَارِ دُونَ أَهْلِ الافْتِكَارِ وَالابْتِكَارِ فَإِنَّ قَلِيلَ ذَلِكَ مَعَ الفِطْنَةِ كَثِيرٌ وَكَثِيرُهُ مَعَ البَلَهِ مُضِرٌّ يَسِيرٌ.

Excessiveness in going deep is blameworthy and the aspiration to delve into amusement is a thing of deprivation, excessive argumentation warrants the enmity of men, spreads turmoil, produces hostility, undermines veneration and increases failure leaving the fledgling without resolve and the expert without a choice for verily Allāh the Most-High is not grasped by understanding and is not conceived by the imagination.

Adhere to seeking the truth and sincerity. Stand by it and do not turn away. Stay away from that which is not necessary for it will require both your concern and regret.

Seek guidance from what I have given you for, out of compassion, I have gone to great lengths to counsel you and it is most correct and rewarding, most sound and adequate and Allāh is most knowing and wise.

This is the last of what we intended regarding a summary of the forebears' traditional creed.

I ask Allāh to benefit whoever reads it, listens to it, or peruses it with a good intention and that He protect us with His munificence and forbearance from every innovated doctrine and make it sincerely for His noble countenance which draws near to Him in the gardens of bliss for indeed He is the Close, the Answerer, the Forbearing, the Merciful. Āmīn.

May peace and prayers be upon our leader Muḥammad, his family, and companions. All praise is for Allāh the Lord of the worlds.

وَالمُمْعِنُ فِي التَّعَمُّقِ مَذْمُومٌ وَالحَرِيصُ عَلَى التَّوَغُّلِ فِي اللَّهْوِ مَحْرُومٌ وَالإِسْرَافُ فِي الجِدَالِ

يُوجِبُ عَدَاوَةَ الرِّجَالِ وَيَنْشُرُ الفِتَنَ وَيُوَلِّدُ الإِحَنَ وَيُقَلِّلُ الهَيْبَةَ وَيُكْثِرُ الخَيْبَةَ فَمَا يَبْقِي

لِمُبْتَدِئٍ قَرَارًا وَلَا لِمِنَّتِهِ اخْتِيَارًا فَإِنَّ اللَّهَ تَعَالَى لَا تَفْهَمُهُ الأَفْهَامُ وَلَا نَتَوَهَّمُهُ الأَوْهَامُ.

فَعَلَيْكَ بِطَلَبِ الحَقِّ الصِّدْقِ وَالوُقُوفِ مَعَهُمَا وَتَرْكِ التَّنْفِيرِ عَنْهُمَا وَاجْتَهِدْ فِي عَدَمِ الدُّخُولِ

فِيمَا لَا يَلْزَمُكَ فَإِنَّهُ يَلْزَمُ مِنْهُ هَمُّكَ وَنَدَمُكَ.

فَاسْتَنْصِحْ يَا أَخِي فِيمَا قَرَّبْتُ إِلَيْكَ وَبَذَلْتُ جُهْدِي فِي نُصْحِكَ شَفَقَةً عَلَيْكَ فَإِنَّهُ أَصْوَبُ

وَأَثْوَبُ وَأَسْلَمُ وَأَقْوَمُ وَأَغْنَمُ وَاللَّهُ أَعْلَمُ وَأَحْكَمُ.

وَهَذَا آخِرُ مَا أَرَدْنَاهُ مِنِ اخْتِصَارِ العَقِيدَةِ السَّلَفِيَّةِ السَّنِيَّةِ.

وَاللَّهَ أَسْأَلُ أَنْ يَنْفَعَ بِهَا مَنْ قَرَأَهَا وَسَمِعَهَا وَطَالَعَهَا بِحُسْنِ النِّيَّةِ وَأَنْ يَعْصِمَنَا بِكَرَمِهِ وَحِلْمِهِ

مِنْ كُلِّ عَقِيدَةٍ بِدْعِيَّةٍ وَأَنْ يَجْعَلَهَا خَالِصَةً لِوَجْهِهِ الكَرِيمِ مُقَرِّبَةً إِلَيْهِ فِي جَنَّاتِ النَّعِيمِ إِنَّهُ

قَرِيبٌ مُجِيبٌ حَلِيمٌ رَحِيمٌ آمِينَ.

وَصَلَّى وَسَلَّمَ عَلَى سَيِّدِنَا مُحَمَّدٍ وَآلِهِ وَصَحْبِهِ أَجْمَعِينَ وَالحَمْدُ لِلَّهِ رَبِّ العَالَمِينَ.

About the Translator

My name is Abu Ibrāhīm John Starling, I am an alumnus of the Islamic University of Madinah. I hold a master's degree in Islamic Studies from the Islamic University of Minnesota and possesses traditional ijāzahs in several subjects including Ḥanbali Fiqh and 'Aqīdah. I have been a student of the Islamic sciences and sought knowledge both formally and traditionally since 2001.

About the Translation

Translating this work and other works of the Ḥanbali School is an honor of a lifetime. For that, all praise and thanks belong to Allāh the Mighty and Sublime.

For this translation I have relied heavily upon the verification and explanation of Shaykh ʿAbdullāh b. Muḥammad AlʿAbdullah. I have also relayed most of his section headings. May Allāh reward him immensely.

During the translation process, I managed to record a brief explanation of the text which I based on several ḥanbali works. These videos are available online and point out the exceedingly rare occasions in which Ibn Balbān differed with Ibn Hamdān or diverged from the authoritative view of the school.

I look forward to your suggestions and corrections so that we, as sincere and loyal disciples, can best represent the works of our tradition.

Join me online at hanbalidisciples.com where you will find other book titles, courses, how-to guides, and a growing repository of questions and answers according to the school.

Printed in Great Britain
by Amazon

41835748R00051